Mind(in)g Me.

MJ RADFORD

Mind(in)g Me.

Overcoming Mental Trials & Reclaiming Positive
Self-Image to Revive Inner Power

Mind(in)g Me. Overcoming Mental Trials & Reclaiming Positive Self-Image to Revive Inner Power Copyright © 2023 by Mylika Radford. All rights reserved.

Published by Poppy Grace Publishing, 34 Shining Willow Way, Suite 391, LaPlata, MD 20646. Poppy Grace books may be bought for educational, business, or sales promotions.

Library of Congress Cataloging-in-Publication Data is available upon request.

Paperback ISBN 979-8-9884295-0-0
Ebook ISBN 979-8-9884295-2-4
Hardcover ISBN 979-8-9884295-1-7

DISCLAIMER: This creative nonfiction work recounts events in my life to the best of my memory. The stories in this book are true, however, some facts have been made sightly fanciful to protect people's privacy and build a strong narrative. I have changed the names, places, times, and details of some characters, in other areas, I condensed two people into one.

Printed in the U.S.A.
FIRST EDITION

Dedication

To my pride and joy, Laia, who brought the
smile back to my son's face.

Acknowledgement

To my Creator, thank you for allowing me to share my story.

Dad and Mom, I love you. You two are the most selfless individuals I know; I am honored to call you parents. Thank you both for always believing in me, encouraging me to be my best self, and for being my greatest teachers.

My son, my "golden child," I am glad that God entrusted you with me. Thank you for your patience as I navigated the bumpy roads of parenthood. I am infinitely grateful for your labor of love, time, and effort you put into this book.

Siblings, thank you for holding me up and keeping me grounded. You three inspire me. I am deeply grateful for your contributions to my literary work—thanks for being among my first readers!

Poppy Grace Publishing team of editors, proofreaders, and designers, your hard work helped transform my publishing dream into reality! To all those who have contributed to my writing journey, whether a little or a lot, I am grateful to you all.

And finally, to the love of my life, James. Thank you for answering the call to love me completely and being my life's partner. Your unwavering encouragement, patience, and understanding is matchless. Your love and support are the bedrock of my strength. Thank you for creating a haven for me to write!

Table of Contents

Origin

"You can't really know where you are going until you know where you have been."

—MAYA ANGELOU

*W*hen I was in the sixth grade, a program called Eye On The Future identified me as a less fortunate student from Detroit's inner city. I was from a marginalized community, a potential statistic, and their program would inspire me to strive for success.

Now, as an adult, I recognize how words like "less fortunate" made me feel less than others.

I recognize how the children who weren't included, who were left behind with a regular Detroit public education, would have felt lesser still.

Most of all, I recognize what "inner city" means. Now I know that's code for where Black people live.

***

Successful people introduced me to the concept of statistics early in life. Statistics were high school dropouts, pregnant teenagers, and drug addicts. The people who populated statistics were the outcasts of society, destined for misfortune and inevitable failure. From my earliest memories, I vowed never to become a statistic.

Statistics were the consumers and sellers of drugs, condemned and compelled to get high, criminal-minded, and lazy. Eye On The Future showed me their pictures in magazines and newspapers. I saw that these women, men, and children carried pain in their eyes, and all too often, they were Black. I did not ask myself if they were just models used to illustrate statistics or if the pictures captured their real lives. Instead, I started associating every brown person with shameful embarrassment, a failure who needed to do better.

The features of these statistical people resembled mine. They had high cheekbones, fuller lips, and button-like noses. The statistics, I deduced, looked like me.

But Eye On The Future corrected me. I was different, they said. I was marginalized. They could help me. They accepted me into their program for the gifted and talented. And so, in the sixth grade, I got caught up in the whirlwind.

When I got older, I learned more about what those labels meant. And despite my ferocious effort to shed them, their words penetrated my core. The well-meaning people who wanted to help, the people who wanted to fix me—they forgot to notice this: nothing was broken inside me.

My family had traditional roles: Mom was a homemaker, and Dad was the breadwinner. My parents raised my siblings and me with strong moral character and a disciplined work ethic. Already by the seventh grade, I knew that single-parent households were inferior, an undesired family structure. The program had taught me not to become a sexually immoral person, one of those downtrodden, young inner-city women with distressed eyes and malnourished children. "Don't Become A Teen Mom!" their brochures screamed. These successful program people, these people from outside of Detroit: they spoke with great authority about our city.

The people from the program framed our experiences and our history through their blurred, subjective lenses. These were the experts who analyzed my world. For five full years, they were the people who called dibs on the driver's seat of my life.

Then, as a junior in high school, I did the unthinkable.

The two blue lines on the pregnancy test I took that Thursday in the 11th grade transformed me from a gifted student who could be helped into one of those sad-eyed people I had seen in magazines and newspapers. Despite all the program's efforts, my future was destined for failure.

Devastation followed. I was a crushing disappointment, not only to my family, but also to the successful people at Eye On The Future. I had become the statistic they had warned me never to become.

For years, I was a passenger in my life, murmuring suggestions to the people up front. Their boisterous viewpoints steered me to a river's edge. Their words sounded suspect to me, but eventually, I stopped trying to correct course. They were all so confident in their ignorance. And I was not.

The views of those successful people shaped my misbeliefs about the world, my people, and even myself. This twisted thinking morphed into years of negative self-image, and it nearly robbed my future. Much later, after I became a lawyer, this revelation devastated me.

There is nothing wrong with Black people. There is nothing wrong with the people from my community in the heart of Detroit. But the message that we are broken fuels this country. This misconception, through Eye On The Future, seeped into my thoughts. Later in life, I learned that my purpose and value stretched beyond labels and identity markers. Somewhere along the way, I had lost confidence. And I was determined to reclaim it.

Today, I deeply desire to become the person God created me to be. I am more aware of my negative self-image and self-sabotaging thoughts. I've also vowed to be gentler and more forgiving to myself. I can't say I've entirely mastered a positive mindset, but I'm improving. To do this, I'm working to cleanse myself of other people's perceptions: those negative images still on constant display in the media, the statistics that still worm their way into my mind.

> **"** Today, I deeply desire to become the person God created me to be!

Mileka Jonson
Detroit, Michigan

1

Comfort in Childhood Simplicities

"Children are likely to live up
to what you believe of them."

—LADY BIRD JOHNSON

*M*y parents were newlyweds in their twenties when they bought the single-family ranch house on Muri Hill Street, one year before I was born. Everything about that red brick home was welcoming. It sang my presence. The gold furniture and red carpet throughout the house had been rolled out for a Royal One named Mileka, whose name means *Queen*. Muri Hill Street always embraced me; it was the source of my stability, and I adored it in return.

Just as I was in the center of our family, eventually the third of four children, our home sat in the center of our block. Its windows overlooked Graham Garden, a massive playground filled with children's freedom and adventure. In that playground, we ran as far as our youthful imaginations could take us.

I was one of many neighborhood kids whose shoes stomped Graham Garden's vivid green grass. We played family baseball games, picking teams to win our annual championship. When we ran across the street to the park, my sister Jayme and I dashed to the monkey bars, while my brother Oto sprinted to the basketball court. There was always a group of kids out on the monkey bars, and Jayme and I joined the gossip of the day. We all ran carefree and wild in that park.

Once our chores were finished, we were free to play, and the Jonson children played harder than most. We knew work came before play. Our parents taught us early in life to take care of our responsibilities before having fun.

11

Every member of the Jonson family had their role, sharing the work of maintaining order at home. To me, our household was orderly and correct: a two-parent family where married parents shared in our upbringing. Dad worked in the paint shop at one of Detroit's Big Three automotive plants. His days were split between the factory where he painted cars, and at "Jim's Enterprises," a beauty supply store he owned on Detroit's East Side. My dad worked non-stop.

By the time he got home after midnight, we kids were in slumberland. We saw him on the weekends at Jim's Enterprises, and when my parents took us on occasional family outings. Dad was missed, but we felt his presence—Mom never let us forget him. She included him in every decision about our lives, which drove me nuts.

"Mom, can I go to my friend's house?"

"You have to ask your dad."

"Can I go on a school field trip?"

"Ask your dad."

That infuriating response lasted well into my teenage years. My mom was consistent, and it wore me out. Even though Dad wasn't always home, he had plenty to say about how his kids were raised.

We all knew Dad was a hard worker, but when he shared the story about him "pickin' cotton at two," my siblings and I felt compelled to get to the bottom of it. Turns out, he actually *did* ride on the back of his older sister's cotton sack. Growing up in tiny Greensboro, Alabama, maintaining a 180-acre plantation, and sharing a tiny house with his parents,

Aneather and Horace, and a dozen siblings taught him the necessity of caring for and appreciating the basics—like food. It may also be why his response to my frequent requests for "fun" was often a no. One time, when I was a sophomore in high school, he finally said yes—and that was the night that changed my life forever.

Mom had the dual role of family and home manager. Just like her mother, Grace, had done before her. Mom supervised every tedious detail of our household. She was the fourth of 12 children and learned to be bossy while helping Grandma Grace keep the younger children in line. Mom was born in Detroit but spent some of her childhood years in Colorado, along with her parents and 11 siblings. At least with all those kids, there was plenty of help with the chores.

That wasn't the case at our house. The three of us kids did everything. Once she was born, we called my little sister Myee "baby girl," and she got away with everything, especially skipping housework. All she needed was to snuggle up to Mom and bat her big brown eyes, and she got anything she ever wanted. I'd been the baby girl before Myee came along, and she booted me from my exalted position.

I'm over that childhood jealousy now. Back then, I had to adjust to my middle-child status. Eventually, I settled in, knowing that the key to keeping my parents happy was completing my chores and doing well in school. Schoolwork came easy—it was the chores that I struggled to manage. I've never been good at keeping things clean and tidy.

My first day of kindergarten is etched in my mind. In the fall of 1983, Mom held my little hand and walked me about four blocks up the street and around the corner to Bow Elementary School. With four main doors on each side of the building, the school occupied about a block's worth of real estate. The kindergartners were assigned the west door, which was closest to our class. When we got there, I gripped Mom's hand, my face pressed into her coat. My heart raced out of my chest. Somehow, I knew that day would change my life.

Before Myee was born, I'd been my parents' youngest child, and when the older kids went to school, I'd had my mother all to myself. But now, I was a big girl in kindergarten. I'd have to muster up the courage to calm my anxiety. I considered throwing a fit, but I knew Mom wouldn't tolerate a tantrum. She bent to kiss my cheek. I hugged her, my only lifeline, kissing my world as I knew it goodbye. I longed to go back home with her, but at the same time, I was curious about that colorful classroom, with numbers, letters, and intriguing images all over the walls. About ten or so other students in the class were taking off their coats, and more parents were waiting to drop off their kids. I released my mom's neck.

"Now remember," she told me, caressing my face with affection. "After school, you wait here for Jayme. She'll take you home when the bell rings."

Then she left. I stood still, my feet planted on the carpet, but my world was spinning like the earth around the sun.

My teacher took my hand and walked me to my cubby partner Atia, the first friend I'd make in school. I was busy taking off my coat, hat, and gloves when another student walked by.

"Hey Four Eyes," he teased.

I just looked at him, stunned and speechless. Then the teacher called everyone to the carpet for class.

The other students ran to the mat, but I had to get rid of "Four Eyes." I tore off my glasses, pushing them to the back of my cubby, behind my coat and backpack. The glasses, I decided, stood in the way of my fitting in. Little did I know that stuffing them into that cubby was the start of the innumerable adjustments I would make to survive in unfamiliar environments as an adult. This day had barely begun, but already it had changed me.

The first day of kindergarten was fun, despite the teasing. I made friends, our teacher was engaging, and the hours flew by. Before I knew it, half-day kindergarten was over. We all ran to our cubbies. I placed my backpack on the floor and put on my coat, hat, and gloves. Then I reached for my glasses.

They were gone.

I dumped everything in my backpack onto the floor, then searched my pockets. *Nothing.*

I rifled through all the other cubbies. *Still nothing.* They were gone. Then I heard my teacher's voice. "Mileka," she called, "Jayme's here for you."

I picked up my bag and made my way to the door, hanging my head so my sister wouldn't see my bare face. "See you tomorrow, Mileka," the teacher waved.

All I could do to wave back, murmuring, "See you tomorrow."

Jayme and I met up with Oto, and we all trudged home together. Neither one of them noticed my missing glasses. But my sense of doom was all-consuming. *What's Mom gonna say?*

> " You have no reason to be ashamed; just be yourself!

When we got home, Mom immediately noticed my bare face, and soon my confession poured out—but I left out the part about "Four Eyes." And Mom surprised me. She didn't fuss at me for losing my glasses. She just made an appointment, and I had new glasses a few days later.

When I wore those new glasses to school, the same kid teased me again. Only this time, I found my five-year-old fire. "You're just mad that *you* don't have glasses," I snapped.

Atia stood up for me, too. She was the first friend who ever came to my defense, and her kindness bolstered my confidence. That day I found my voice—but the challenge would be to hang onto it.

My parents helped, too. "You have no reason to be ashamed, Mileka," my mother reassured me. "Those glasses look beautiful on you. Just be yourself!" I have a sneaking suspicion why she never scolded me for losing them. Somehow, I think she knew I'd been teased. Not for nothing she'd been raising Jayme and Oto before me—that woman just *knew* things.

"Be yourself, Mileka." I returned to that early childhood lesson frequently over the years. But Mom's lessons weren't always so direct. She also taught us through poems. One of my favorites was "The Little Elf."

"I met a little elf man once
Down where lilies blow.
I asked him why he was so small
And why he would not grow.
He slightly frowned and with his eyes,
He looked me through and through.
'I'm quite as big for me,' he said,
'As you are big for you.'"

—John Kendrick Bangs

The first day of kindergarten was scary, but after Day One, I was sold. Library, art, gym, and social studies were my favorite subjects, and in those classes, I discovered my life's interests. Social studies showed me how to think critically about the world's people. Our art teacher inspired our creativity and discipline. He gave us room to explore our underlying potential while guiding us to shape our ideas into masterpieces. My gym teacher, Ms. Scott, believed in me, instilling in me the expectation of doing my very best. When I wimped out on our sit-ups, my abs on fire, she made me finish my set. And, of course, the library was bursting with inspiration. I loved sitting in a circle on the carpet while the librarian read to us. She always flipped her book around to show us the illustrations, and what adventures lay between those pages!

Once the school day finished and we all came home, the Jonson household transformed into a learning center. Mom made it fun, especially the after-school activities. Every day she designed treasure hunts for us, scattering notes throughout the house with clues for each step. The prize was always a bag of gold (okay, silver dollars, fifty-cent pieces, and quarters!) awarded to the first kid who found it. The competition was thick because Mom often kept my cousins, Atiba and Akili, who were eager to find that treasure, too.

Now that I look back, I realize how time-consuming it must have been for Mom to design those treasure hunts, but she did it anyway, realizing that all work and no play would make us dull children. My mother's learning games sparked my imagination, and reading with her became a daily adventure. She had us take turns reading out loud, and that's when the real fun started. When someone mispronounced a word, we all tittered—until Mom glared at us for laughing at other people's slip-ups. If there's one thing Mom didn't tolerate, it was rudeness.

At our house, my mother crafted adventures with words. Whenever we were intrigued by a word or a question, Mom directed us to "look it up."

"Mom, how do clouds make lightning?"

"Look it up."

"Why do some birds hop and some birds fly?"

"Look it up."

"What are atoms made of?"

"I told you, *look it up.*"

She encouraged us to be independent thinkers and self-contained, while also urging us to care for one another. That's why I often sought out my brother or sister to help me with words that confused me, and none of us ever had to feel embarrassed for asking.

Not to brag, but I had everything I needed as a child. We all had plenty of clothes and toys. And while our tribe of adults may have spoiled us, Mom made sure we didn't grow up into spoiled brats. She knew exactly how to strike a balance.

Mom divided our chores among us, and there were enough to keep anyone busy around the clock. Two of us worked in the kitchen, one had to scrub out the bathroom, and the last one had to vacuum the floors. We sometimes fought over who would wash the dishes because none of us wanted wrinkly hands, plus the water always splashed our clothes. Drying was an easy job, but I hardly ever got that one. That might be why I still detest doing the dishes, even to this day.

My parents taught me tenacity at a very young age. I suppose I have them to thank for my workaholism. Mom kept up with the kids, whereas my father was always on the job. He left for his evening shift just before we got home from school, and he didn't get home until after midnight. So we only got to spend time with him on weekends, when he supervised us cutting the grass and manicuring the garden. Ugh! I hate to say this, but I was not a fan of yard work. Rain or shine, Dad woke us up early every Saturday to get out in the garden and work. It was miserable. To him, it was family time, but for me, it was ghastly. Even though we hated it, we got up and got it done. So that's where my strong work ethic comes from—even today, I stick it out, even when I can't stand the job.

As the African proverb says, "It takes a village to raise a child," and that rang true on Detroit's West Side. In elementary, our principal was stern. Dr. Graysen's bulky, seven-foot frame could be intimidating. But he was also jovial, funny, sincere, impartial, and unbiased. Of course, corporal punishment was still allowed in school back then, and when we broke the rules, we got paddled.

I was determined never to end up on the wrong side of that paddle—until one day, it turned on me. I got caught clowning around in class, and my favorite teacher smacked me on the backside. That was the first and last time I got walloped at school. I managed to make it through elementary school with very few instances of trouble.

After fifth grade graduation, I joined my friends chanting Bow's anthem as my right of passage to junior high:

"Bow, Bow
we're cheering for you
Don't get us wrong we mean to be true
In spite of workbooks, pens and rules
We love you, our own Bow school!"

2

Bittersweet Coffey

"Children must be taught how
to think, not what to think."

–MARGARET MEAD

*O*nce I graduated from Bow Elementary and went on to Coffey Middle School, life got a little more complicated. The first challenge I had to confront was the scourge of the strict dress code.

"Mileka, you need to go to the counselor's office at once," my homeroom teacher ordered one day in first period. I was just getting settled in my seat.

I gaped at him. "What did I do?"

"You're out of dress code. "

I rolled my eyes. *Not again.* I shoved things into my bag, mumbling words of hatred toward my teacher. *It's the culottes again, I know it.* All sixty eyes were on me, and I needed to get out of sight ASAP.

I strolled down the center aisle of the class, pretending to be perfectly calm and unbothered. I knew my classmates would tease me forever if I ever let up on my poker face.

Once I was out in the hallway however, my stoic face melted into distress. Despite my defiance, the truth was that I *wanted* to be in class, not facing Ms. Rearden, the stern counselor who was paid to make students' lives miserable. By the time I got to the office, I had refined my defense. I was ready to plead my case.

"The pants are inappropriate, which is an absolute violation of the school's dress code," Ms. Rearden warned me. "If you keep breaking the rules like this, you leave me no other choice than to suspend you."

I shot her a resentful look. "Huh?"

"No long shorts in school, Mileka; your bottoms need to cover your ankles."

"If I can make myself clear, these are not shorts. They are culottes," I snarked.

She glared at me, and we stared each other down. Eventually, I snapped.

"I want to call my mom," I blurted.

Surprisingly, she placed the phone in front of me without a word. It rang three times before Mom picked up.

"Hey, Ma." I explained how the teacher had unjustly yanked me out of class and exiled me to the counselor's office. But before I could finish my tale of woe, Ms. Reardon gestured at me to hang up the phone. *Insane lady!*

Minutes later, Mom showed up in the office. "What seems to be the problem?" she asked briskly, extending her hand to the counselor.

Ms. Reardon explained that my ankles were scandalously exposed.

My mother took a seat. "I assure you, Ms. Reardon," she began, "that I approved Mileka's outfit before she left for school. And wouldn't you agree the students should remain in class, learning, rather than spending their time discussing their fashion choices?"

Ms. Reardon sputtered something about school policy.

"Personally," my mother continued, "I think the school should revise their dress code to avoid unnecessarily pulling children out of class. Nevertheless," and at this she placed a brown paper bag on the desk, "I have brought a change of clothes for Mileka."

Really, Mom? That was a bummer. I thought she was on my side here!

But there was no fighting it. This was Mom's way of teaching me to respect adults, follow the rules, and compromise—even if it meant taking off my pretty culottes.

At the time, it seemed like the school was always picking on what we girls chose to wear. But now that I look back on it, I see there was more to the story than just arbitrary supervising of our fashion choices. They might have been trying to protect us. At least one female classmate I knew was attacked, assaulted, and brutally raped while walking to school in the wee hours of the morning. But at the time, I didn't care about their rationale. I felt picked on for wearing culottes, and no one could convince me otherwise.

Other than the occasional skirmish around dress codes, I enjoyed middle school as much as elementary. Ms. Greer drew us in with her deep, crisp voice, broad vocabulary, and ability to teach history in a relatable way. When the lesson started, I'd sit at my desk with my chin resting in my hands, and slowly my favorite stories began to liberate my mind.

Ms. Greer relayed the history of slavery. She told us how some enslaved people fought for their freedom and rights, while others remained in bondage.

Then she asked, "Why is that?"

"They didn't know they could fight and free themselves from tyrants," called out one of the students. Then one by

25

one, we all chimed in with our answers. Ms. Greer nodded but never indicated which answer was correct.

"What else?" she prompted, placing one wrist over the other as though her hands were tied. Then she ripped them apart. "We are no longer chained here," she declared. "We must be sure to never let our minds be bound."

Although I didn't know it then, my worldview was being shaped in Room 301.

As much as I loved Mrs. Greer's history class, the most important lessons at Coffey Middle School were learned outside the classroom. One day, in the school cafeteria, my arch-enemy Kassidy kicked me hard in the shins.

"Watch yourself, Kassidy!" I yelled at her.

"I didn't kick you on purpose," she protested. "You need to calm down."

That just made me angrier, and I slapped her before she could duck away. Eventually, the teachers broke us up, but that wasn't the end of it—not by a long shot. When the bell for dismissal rang at the end of the day, a bunch of kids started following me around, chanting, "Fight! Fight! Fight!"

I didn't need much encouragement. I was sick of Kassidy's bullying and smack talk. So when Jason dared me to knock the stick off her shoulder, I slapped it right off.

She whirled around and punched me, and we kicked, scratched, and flailed until our teacher pulled us apart. I was declared the winner, although my shiner told a different story.

Cocky in my victory, I was hauled into the counselor's office again, this time for fighting. And once the adrenaline wore off, I started fretting. *Who's going to walk through that door? Mom? Dad? What are they going to do to me?*

I was nauseous, and I admit I was a little petrified.

In the end, neither of my parents came in. Instead, Ms. Lindsey entered the room. And instead of asking about the fight, she said, "Have you seen your sister Jayme?"

Jayme? Why is she asking me about Jayme?

Ms. Lindsey walked me down the never-ending hallway to her office. On the way, we passed an older man staggering on the stairs near the principal's office in a pair of stained pants. He had grass in his hair and he smelled like gin.

When I saw my sister, my heart dropped. "Jayme!?" She was sitting there, wincing in pain, with a colossal bump swelling on her forehead. "What happened?"

The principal soon explained. Turns out, after our fight, a classmate went to get Kassidy's father. And he came to defend her, all right—he stumbled onto the school's property swinging a billy club. He was after anyone and everyone who was associated with *me,* so he smashed Jayme, my friend Althea, and her little sister before anyone could stop him. Eventually, some of the older brothers who picked up their siblings from school saw him attacking the students and fought him off. And that was the guy—the sad, drunk man I'd seen in the corridor.

At that moment, I understood Kassidy a bit better. I felt terrible for fighting her and not finding some other way to work things out. Maybe she was a bully because she lived with a drunk and violent father. Chances were, his rage turned on her at home.

Eventually, my sister's forehead healed up, but Kassidy had to live with that incident for months. Her father was criminally charged for attacking my sister and friends, and Kassidy had to endure all the gossip for the rest of the year. She avoided me whenever I saw her outside of school.

I won that fight, but later I felt awful about how she shrank from me on the street. I didn't want to be a violent person, lashing out at people who were already hurt. That day in the cafeteria led me to a place of greater compassion. And I still have very little tolerance for bullying to this day.

My fight with Kassidy was almost the worst thing that happened to me in middle school. It took second place to the death of my seventh-grade friend, Henry Nolan, who was hit by a car riding his bike across busy Greenfield Road. I cried for a week straight. My classmates and I were shattered. Henry's death brought us closer, and cherishing my friends became my most valuable adolescent lesson.

Towards the end of middle school, I found my groove. I loved participating in classes that stretched my creativity. Drama class was an unmatched favorite because it introduced me to the creativity of my culture. We performed everything from *The Wiz* to plays about civil rights, and once I even got to play Rosa Parks. My most memorable performance was dancing a solo to "Black Butterfly." I felt that song in my soul. With every plié and twirl, I built a lasting self-confidence and belief that I, Black Butterfly, flying across the stage in my leotard, was unstoppable.

At Coffey Middle School, I flapped my wings and soared into creativity and artistic expression. It left me curious about the world. And that's when I was identified by Eye On The Future as a "student of talent." Once they enrolled select students in the program, they took us on field trips to museums and college visits. Then they sat us down and started teaching us about statistics.

From those pictures, I inferred that Black people were more likely to be on drugs, drop out of school, and have broken families due to abusive husbands, rebellious children, or philandering wives.

"Are we that bad?" I thought to myself.

Those discussions frightened me. No one talked about *how* people ended up on the margins of society. Rather, it was as though failure was their inevitable lot in life. My takeaway from those sessions was a single sentence: *Mileka, do not be a statistic.*

> **"** I hid my true self for decades, adding veil after veil of flawed thoughts until I was entirely shrouded. I was good at playing my role, but bit by bit, my spirit was dying.

To achieve my goal, I worked harder. I would rise above my community. I couldn't change what people thought about us in general, but I had control over what people thought of *me*. Most importantly, to avoid becoming a Black statistic, I knew I had to hide who I was.

I must say, I did an excellent job. I hid my true self for decades, adding veil after veil of flawed thoughts until I was entirely shrouded. I was good at playing my role, but bit by bit, my spirit was dying. My words ghosted me. I stopped exploring the arts. I did everything I could not to be myself. All I knew was that I had to be better than the Mileka God had created.

This corrupt, self-sabotaging thinking echoed in my thoughts for decades. Not until my mid-thirties did I begin to discover the innate being I was destined to be. She is genuine, loving, lovable, and created in the image of God.

And even now, I wonder about those lessons they taught in Eye On The Future. That the people who look like me are failures. That I must transform myself into a "good" person. That I must distance myself from my roots. That I should strive to be someone I am not.

And if, as a child, I had asked them, "What are you teaching?"

I still wonder what they would have said.

3

High School Woes

"Rebellion is when you look society in the
face and say I understand who you want
me to be, but I'm going to show you who
I actually am."

—ANTHONY ANAXAGOROU

*T*here were three top public high schools in Detroit at that time, and the one that was closest to me was Renaissance High. You had to take an entrance test to get in. I did well, but I missed the qualifying grade by a single point. That meant it was Henry Ford High School for me.

I was a high-achieving student in high school. In fact, my failure to get into Renaissance pushed me into overdrive. From that moment onward, I signed up for all the most challenging classes I could find, even enrolling in college-level coursework. Track, JROTC, and newspaper were my extracurricular activities, and I also worked part-time jobs at Wendy's and a nursing home. I didn't even take a break during my one free period, instead working in the office as a student administrator. I loved high school and most of the teachers were great, especially Mr. Colby, the Assistant Principal. He was relatable and cool, standing six feet tall, and always dressed in an immaculate suit. He encouraged and mentored me, and I revered him.

My hectic schedule lasted until the end of my eleventh-grade year, and at that point, I burned out. No teenage fun was happening to me, and I was determined to change that. So, I tagged along with Jayme who'd managed to get out of our strict household for the afternoon.

One Saturday in August, we went to Northland Mall, then met friends at the movie theatre. It was the teenage hot spot. After we watched a movie, we hung around with some friends for a bit then headed back to our car. That's when one of the guys caught my eye. His flirtatious advances felt weird and intriguing. Finally, my interest won out and I accepted the ripped paper he pressed into my hand. It had his beeper number on it, and I promised to page him.

Antony was tall, dark, and handsome, and most importantly, he took an interest in me. I loved his easy laugh and go-getter mentality. He was the first guy I chatted with on the phone for hours, and he was also my very first date. Somehow I managed to get a "yes" from Dad when I asked to go out with Antony. He promised to have me back home at 7 pm, but I made sure that didn't happen.

Antony and I were enjoying the evening, and I begged him not to take me back home. He eventually gave in and that night, I lost my childhood innocence and got pregnant. Once I found out what had happened, I was utterly lost and angry with myself for making such a poor decision. I tried to keep my pregnancy a secret, but as I've mentioned, my mom is a woman of intuition. The day after I saw those two blue lines on the pregnancy test, she asked me when I'd last had my cycle.

"Why would you ask me that?" I snapped defensively. But I think she knew.

Either way, I wasn't about to accept my fate. Instead, I applied to the court for an abortion. At the time, minor girls in Michigan needed either parental consent or a court order to have a legal abortion. I chose to face the judge rather than my parents. Thankfully, I was successful. Antony told me he thought it was the wrong decision, but I didn't care. I had my mind made up.

Then I felt my son move in my belly. And I knew I couldn't go through with it.

Mom and Dad had always told us they'd kick us out if we got pregnant, so I was terrified to confess.

"Mmm-hmm," my mom said, sounding totally unsurprised. "You need to tell your dad."

But surprisingly, Dad was tremendously more supportive than I expected him to be. For one thing, he didn't kick me out of the house right away.

Months went by, and I followed my everyday routine of attending classes and extracurricular activities. But I was no longer the prodigy, the girl who would make Henry Ford High School proud. I was a pregnant teenager before teen moms were popular. I was a statistic.

One day during class change, I saw Mr. Colby in the first-floor hallway. He was moving students along, stopping any horseplay before the bell rang. Then he signaled me to stop.

"Mileka," he said, "I need to ask you. Are you pregnant?"

I looked down, my face burning with embarrassment, the other students bustling around us. Finally, I couldn't avoid it. "Yes, Mr. Colby," I told him. "I'm due in December."

"Oh, Mileka," he said softly. "You have no idea how much you've messed up your life. All that work...what a waste."

His words rang in my ears for quite a time. Mr. Colby had labeled me as a disappointment and a failure. I left that conversation crushed.

That was the last day I spoke to the Assistant Principal. He ignored me daily until the end of the school year. I was hurt, but I tried to hide it. I chalked it up to just one more person who was no longer in my corner. In his eyes, I was not the same student he'd mentored. I doubt he cared, but in my eyes, he changed too.

I didn't always manage to hide my feelings. We had security guards at our school, and one of the first things that happened when word got around about my condition is that they started putting lots of energy into making my life difficult. One morning I rushed into school at 5:55, almost late for my 6:00 am pre-college class, and hurried through the metal detector. Without a beep sounding, the security guard snatched my cross-body bag, opened it, and started combing through it.

My blood was boiling like sulfur in hell. I grabbed my bag from her grip. "There isn't anything in my purse, and you know it!" I told her. "We go through this every morning, and I'm tired of it."

Speechless, she stared at me.

"You know I'm in the pre-college class. Regular school starts at eight o'clock in the morning. Why else in the world would I be here so early?"

And that's when she let loose. "You unruly, hardheaded little kid. Do you think you're going to college like that? Dream on missy, *dream on.*"

I turned and walked away, already late for my class, but this woman was right on my heels and screaming in my ears. "Maybe you wouldn't be pregnant in the first place if you followed the *rules* every once in a while!"

"Leave me *alone,*" I managed to say, already close to tears. I made it to the door of my classroom and opened it.

"Yeah? Maybe that boyfriend of yours should have left you alone! You hardheaded, disrespectful little—"

Every head in the class turned toward me as the security guard's words drowned out the teacher's voice. "Sorry," I muttered, mortified. I lowered my eyes, reached for my book, and slumped into my seat as the teacher redirected everyone's attention to the lesson.

The conflicts increased after that day, mainly with the adults at school. One day in my seventh month of pregnancy, I found I couldn't perch on the high metal stools in the biology lab, so Ms. Patel kicked me out of class, sending me to the Assistant Principal's office for being "turbulent."

But when I knocked on his door, Mr. Colby just sighed and turned his back on me, like there was nothing more he could do. That really crushed my spirit. It was like I no longer existed to him.

It seemed like almost all the adults lost any respect they ever had for me. They didn't know what to make of me, the lost, promised child. And I felt it. *Is it that bad to have a baby?* I asked myself, honestly perplexed at how completely my world had changed. I wondered about that for a long time.

And I could have used some adult support. I was scared of the unknown, and how my life was about to unwind. My dream of going to Spelman had been tossed aside, and I had no way of knowing what the future would hold. The only peace I got was my after-school naps.

I slumbered into la-la land, praying to God: *Please let me have a healthy child. Please let me be a good mother. Please let me graduate on time.* Those were my only supplications during those months of uncertainty.

A couple of teachers did show me grace. Ms. Bens, my Calculus II teacher, encouraged me to stay focused and finish high school. One day after class, she asked to talk to me. *Here we go,* I thought, *another lecture.* I braced myself as she opened her desk drawer and pulled out a little gift bag.

"Mileka, I'm proud of you," she said.

I shook my head, thinking I'd heard her wrong. "You are?"

"Yes. I know it hasn't been easy for you, to stay on top of schoolwork while you're pregnant. And I know you'll do great things because you're determined and focused."

My eyes welled up with tears as I realized she hadn't given up on me. "Aww, thank you, Ms. Bens."

"You're going to be a great mother and your son is blessed to have you. Things may get difficult for you with juggling college, but keep your eyes straight ahead and focused—just like you have in my class."

Then she handed me the blue gift bag, and I allowed myself to be free and vulnerable at that moment. Finally, someone saw me for who I was and what I was trying to do. In the bag was a happy baby figurine. That small gift meant so much to me. It showed me that precious things could be born from life's biggest mistakes.

My 12th Grade Homecoming wasn't exactly what I'd dreamed of, but it was still exciting. I purchased a peach pants suit from the maternity section of Marshall Fields, and my hair was in an updo, complimenting my natural tone makeup and extra-long artistic nails. I *loved* those nails. The other students danced all night, while I stayed on the sidelines massaging my achy, swollen feet. But I didn't mind. I still felt beautiful.

Then, on a frosty evening at the end of December, my handsome son Taven was born. At that moment, I knew anything was possible...except enduring more labor pains! Little Taven was a miracle to me. God had entrusted his sweet, innocent, and precious life with my seventeen years of experience in this world, and I was determined not to fail. I would raise this child well, in a manner that would please God.

After my son was born, more people pitched in to support me. My father volunteered to babysit Taven during the school day. My guidance counselor, Mr. Kulnis, helped to arrange my schedule around my baby. The few times I missed school, he collected my work from my teachers for me. He joined my commitment to graduating on time. And Ms. Bens, my lovely Black Calculus teacher, always stood in my corner. Whenever I started feeling discouraged, she pulled me to the side and

> **"** My teenage world vanished with motherhood, but I stayed focused on my goals...I wasn't sure of myself, who I was, or what I was becoming. But nothing and no one would stand in the way.

gave me a quick pep talk about staying in the fight until graduation.

My teenage world vanished with motherhood, but I stayed focused on my goals. Maybe I wasn't the promised child anymore. Maybe I wasn't sure of myself, who I was, or what I was becoming. But nothing and no one would stand in the way of me walking across that stage.

Six months after Taven was born, on June 5, 1996, I walked across the stage with honors at Detroit's Cobo Hall. I graduated high school on time, making my prayers come true. However, what I would do afterward was still a huge question mark. Aspiring to attend Spelman was out of mind and out of reach. Now, I planned to create a stable life by getting the bare necessities for my modest family under control.

But that was easier said than done. Being a teenager was confusing enough without adding parenthood into the mix. And I still had those words echoing in my head, the echoes that told me I was *hardheaded. Wasted. Ruined.*

4

Motherhood Fumbles

"Nothing happens until you decide. Make a decision and watch your life move forward."

−OPRAH

*H*aving my son made me feel grown-up, but I was still a teenager living with my parents. Soon after high school, I started defying their household rules. Staying out all night became my routine. Mom warned me that if I pulled another all-nighter, she would no longer let me live under her roof. She was clear and direct, but I was determined to push the limits.

A few weeks after her warning, I stayed out all night again. Early the following day, I left Antony's house and came back home. Dad was half-asleep when he opened the door for me. My mom had already left for work.

As I walked shamelessly to my room, I heard Dad's groggy voice. "Your mom left you a note," he said.

"Okay," I replied.

That's a weird thing to mention, I thought, *but whatever.*

When I got to my room, all my belongings were gone. In the corner were two suitcases packed with my things, a note perched on top. The handwritten letter was loving but austere:

Mileka,

I have warned you repeatedly, but you refuse to follow the rules of our home. Taven can stay, but you cannot live here anymore. Please be gone before I return home today.

Love, Mom.

43

I dropped the letter and flounced out of the room. "Dad? DAD!" I burst into my parents' bedroom and pleaded with him, but it was an utter waste of time. The two of them were a united front.

Furious, I grabbed my baby with all my bags, and stormed out of the house. My rebellious heart stung with the thought of my parents turning their backs on me. *Supportive? Ha! I thought you wanted to help, not kick me out on the street!* I started up my little red Saturn and sped down Muri Hill, tears streaming down my cheeks. Consumed with feelings of righteous rage, I was blind to my fault in the matter. After all, she *had* warned me. I hadn't intended to break my parent's rules, but I loved Antony. Our oil and water relationship was not mixing well. But despite our lack of experience, I still hoped we could make it work and form a family of our own.

Years later, I grasped my mother's rationale. She still had Myee to raise, and she couldn't risk having a disobedient child in the house, modeling an example of blatant disrespect. Unfortunately, getting kicked out was the beginning of a downward spiral in my life. It would be a long time before I came back to myself.

Instead of examining my own actions, I ran to the only person in the world I thought could understand me: Antony. Together with our baby, living in his mother's house, we'd magically learn to be adults together. We'd live happily ever after.

That fantasy was short-lived. We were just a couple of feuding teenagers, trying to find our way. Living with his mother wasn't a long-term solution. The warm glow of young love faded with the pressures of real life. My constant demands that 17-year-old Antony step into a grown man's shoes were unrealistic. We both felt doomed and ill-equipped to face the challenges ahead.

The next two years of my life were a constant battle. My living situation was in flux. Refusing to return home to face my failures, I found myself homeless, with no place to go. My cousin Charmane was kind enough to take me in, and I stayed on her smooth hardwood floor for a while. She had two children around Taven's age, so it worked out for a while—but we weren't stable. Eventually, I got another waitressing job, so I had money to support us—or at least contribute to Charmane's household.

Then my older sister Jayme came to the rescue. In early 1997, she moved back from Ohio. She found a house to rent with my aunt, and there were two bedrooms in the bottom unit. I could have the second one if I wanted it. *Of course!*

Things were starting to look up.

Working as a waitress and bartender, I stacked my tips. I had enough money to pay my bills and even a little extra to spend a night out with the girls or splurge on the occasional pamper day. I finally had a stable home and a car that Jayme and I shared. But still, I yearned for something more. A four-year college degree seemed out of the question with a three-year-old son to support, so I focused on getting a quick qualification to earn more money.

One day after work, I saw a commercial on TV that told me I could get my paralegal degree in under a year. Almost everyone was accepted, and with that degree in hand, I'd have valuable professional skills. That commercial lit a fire in me. I called the program instantly, registered for classes, and in a few weeks, I was a paralegal student! Even my family was back on board to support me. My parents and Antony's family would take care of Taven while I was working and in classes.

By enrolling in paralegal training, I was well on my way to rising above the statistics, and in my very first semester, I found my flow. Each morning, I dropped my son off at my parents' house and headed up to school, listening to my own thoughts since the radio in my Nissan Maxima was broken. Ironically, my CD player worked when I played "Keep Ya Head Up" by Tupac. I was fed up with how my life was going, but Tupac's song gave me hope that things would get better. Once I arrived, I sat in a class of about 15 people, most of whom were older than me. There weren't very many Black people, but everyone was nice in their own way. The material came naturally to me, and I was quick to raise my hand to offer my perspective on most topics.

> **"** One tiny goal kept my mind clear and my eyes on the future.

Of course, learning how to be a paralegal was a long way from being a lawyer, but that one tiny goal kept my mind clear and my eyes on the future.

5

Finding My Way

"Just because my path is different doesn't mean I'm lost."

—GERARD ABRAMS

*N*avigating motherhood took grace. It was a balancing act. Earning money for my family was on one side of the scale, and the other side was weighed down by my responsibility to love and care for my son. That last part was the side that always seemed to lack. Despite my best efforts, I constantly felt that I came up short as a mother. I wanted Taven to have the best life possible, even though I'd nearly choked off my own chance at success. Very little, it seemed, was under my control.

The first few months of paralegal training were a blur of minimum-wage jobs, making just enough money to put cheap meals in front of us. When my meager paychecks waitressing and temping didn't cover the bills, I did what so many others do—I got another low-paying job. That was not an easy choice, because it meant spending even more hours away from Taven. When I did get to spend time with him, my sleep deprivation resulted in my being a short-tempered mom. In hindsight, I missed many opportunities to enjoy being in the moment with my child. During the years I toiled to make a better life for us, I knew I was missing life's treasures with the person God had entrusted to me.

Thankfully, I knew I wasn't in this thing alone. I rejected the "single mother" phrase. My circle of support kept me striving. Even after they kicked me out of the house, Dad and Mom were always in my corner, and their home remained welcoming and open to us. Antony's mother watched Taven to give me a break on some weekends. His great-grandparents always asked to keep him as well. There was no shortage of family love around us. After all, it does take a village.

At the end of my second semester in paralegal school, I was more than halfway through the program—but then the money problems hit. Most of my tuition was free if I maintained a 3.0 GPA, but for some reason, there was always a balance left over at the end of each semester. My minimum wage job and waitress tips only got me so far. One day at the end of May, I looked at the $500 tuition bill and decided I'd rather pay my rent. That was my choice. The program had already taught me a few skills, so I figured I'd cut my losses and look for a job.

I submitted my resume to a staffing company and waited anxiously for a callback. Weeks passed, and the phone didn't ring. Then one day, a recruiter called and told me that someone wanted to interview me.

Man, was I excited to finally get a break! That tuition debt was weighing heavily on my shoulders, and this was the first job I'd ever applied to that paid more than minimum wage. *Maybe*, I thought, *with a little bit of luck, this will lead to even better opportunities down the line.*

The day came for the interview, and I drove forty-five minutes from Detroit to Troy. I went in for my appointment at the national headquarters for King Crafts. It quickly became clear that I wasn't qualified for the job, but Angela, the lead attorney, who was nearly my complexion and about ten years my senior, gave me a chance. She saw promise in me. Maybe I still had a little twinkle in my eye left from high school.

To this day I don't know how I won her over. Maybe she saw my pain and wanted to help me work through it, but whatever the reason, she rolled the dice and hired me as her legal assistant. She told me so right on the spot, just after the interview. I was *elated*. This was the whole reason I'd enrolled in paralegal school in the first place: to get an excellent-paying job. Although the position was temporary, I felt like I was well on my way to defying the statistics. That was the day I learned *never* to count myself out.

On Day One, it was all business. Angela was very stern and settled for nothing but the highest standards. Everything about that office environment was new to me, but I was willing to do whatever it took to stay there. And I did. That short-term position lasted for almost five years. It eventually turned into a full-time, permanent job, with full benefits.

> 66 Seeing those bright young people gave me the vision to know I could do the same.

During the time I worked for her, Angela taught me about professionalism. She taught me everything from basic computer skills to managing the litigation charts for all the outside counsel. Angela was the president of a specialty bar organization, and I helped with some of her events and board meetings, sometimes attending them myself.

One evening, I accompanied Angela to a law student reception that was being held at the lavish home of a local judge. Most of the law students were around my age, some slightly older, and seeing them planted a little seed in my head about going back to school. Seeing those bright young people gave me the vision to know I could do the same. And the lawyers seemed so wise to me: intelligent, eloquent, and fueled with purpose.

I was sold—not just on the judge's lavish home, but on the camaraderie between Black professionals. Those lawyers and judges spoke about things that were a bit over my head sometimes, but they made me want to achieve more with my life. The host had a library in his house, and when I saw those rows of books, I felt the same joy I had as a child, sitting on the library floor at Bow Elementary. I longed for my very own library one day, with a ladder to reach the books way up near the ceiling.

I yearned for the lifestyle of those accomplished professionals because everyone seemed so happy and passionate about what they were doing in their lives. And Angela must have noticed my interest, because she started nagging me daily about applying to college. But before I could expand outward, I needed to find more stability in my personal life.

Every evening, once I clocked out, I entered a world of chaos. My relationship with Antony was crumbling. The more I talked about going back to college, the more he felt rejected and competitive with me. He accused me of trying to better myself to leave him. We argued constantly. Our scuffles started early in the morning, and they often made me late for work. At one point, our endless feuding nearly cost me my job.

That's when I knew I had to end it. Being a mother and a working professional was hard enough. College would make things even more difficult. And there was no room in my life for drama.

6

Lost

"Not until we are lost do we begin to
understand ourselves."

-HENRY DAVID THOREAU

"Wow, *that's* special!"
"So fancy! Is that your *real hair*?"
"Can I touch it?"

*D*uring those years at King Crafts, nothing set me apart from my colleagues more decisively than my hair. Barely out of my teens, I didn't know how to dress or style myself for the office. I was the youngest person and one of the few Black people in the legal department. Eventually, I learned to dress "professionally," but I had a lot of ground to make up for.

I had just started finding my style when I got pregnant at 17. I starting wearing the baggiest things I could get to conceal my growing baby bump. After I had my son, I wore whatever was comfortable. Now, in my early twenties, I wanted to have fun with style again—but those cute '90s outfits didn't conform to a corporate setting. And then there was my hair dilemma.

The first time I styled my hair like a 20-year-old, with curly extensions, I strode into the office full of confidence—and my co-workers stared like my head was on fire. It was ridiculous. Defending my hair became a daily occurrence.

Each comment about my appearance or attempt to touch my hair as if we were in a petting zoo added to my collection of insecurities.

Eventually, I started conforming to blend in with my white counterparts. After all, they were the self-professed "majority," and who wouldn't want to be on their team, right? I reasoned that they were on top because they knew how things worked and had it all figured out. I now know this was a very destructive way of thinking. Nonetheless, I learned to adapt, making a concerted effort to blend in. How silly was I to believe that I, Mileka, whose name means Queen, could blend in? More importantly, why would I *want* to blend in? Erasing my individuality just served to stop me from bringing it or giving *my* best self to the world. Bit by bit, those attempts to conform eroded the very fabric of my being, and it would take decades for me to find myself again.

Two years after I joined King Crafts, Angela announced she was leaving the company. I was happy for her, but the ensuing office chatter made me nervous. "What are you going to do now?" people asked, genuinely curious. They may not have meant to, but their questions pierced my confidence. It was clear they thought of me as Angela's "project," and that I wouldn't survive in the office without her.

I was reassured when Angela cut in to answer their questions for me. "She's going to do what anyone would," she replied. "*Work.*"

Angela's retort let me know that, regardless of how close we were, she respected me as an individual in charge of my own professional destiny. She'd brought me into the company, but my success there was up to me.

With Angela gone, my focus was on continuing my journey to a higher purpose, finishing college, and working. Two years after she left, King Crafts slowly began to downsize. At one point I was one of two in the department. To stay on top of the work, I dragged three-year-old Taven to the empty office with me on Saturdays. Back then there was no iPad to keep him busy, so I gave him a stack of typing paper to draw on. Before he got antsy, I emptied a bag of rubber bands and let him wrap them around my rubber band ball. Afterward, he bounced that ball up and down the office. This routine ended when one day, the CEO knocked on my cuBIC le and called me into his office, letting me know that my job would be eliminated.

> 66 Erasing my individuality just served to stop me from bringing it or giving my best self to the world. Bit by bit, those attempts to conform eroded the very fabric of my being, and it would take decades for me to find myself again.

Part of me was relieved because now I would have time to focus on my son and finish school, but I also knew losing my job would leave me broke. Luckily, they offered a small severance package. That financial cushion helped me to finish the year as a full-time student.

And as for my mentor Angela, we kept in touch. She vowed that she would be there for me every step of the way—

through college graduation, acceptance to law school, law school graduation, passing the bar exam, and beyond. She kept her promise.

7

Job-Free

"Being broke is a temporary situation.
Being poor is a state of mind."

—MIKE TODD

*B*eing job-free had its difficulties. I struggled to pay my bills, and my pride kept me from asking my parents for much more than they had already given me. After all, at that point I was living in a house my parents purchased for their children, and they were charging me minimal rent.

Between an assortment of part-time jobs, I managed to pay the utilities and phone, maintain the property, take care of my son, and ensure that we both were fed. Every skill set I'd learned up until then was devoted to making a living. I did hair, cleaned houses, and made festivity baskets. Whatever anyone needed, I offered my services for a reasonable fee. Many different business propositions were presented to me, some of them less than legal. I was tempted by the easy cash, but my values kept me on course.

Being broke sucked, but I always had everything I needed. During semester breaks I enjoyed time with my Taven, and I volunteered for a few days at his school. I enjoyed that downtime from work. It made me a better homemaker. Gardening, cooking, and enjoying the pleasures of just being were delightful.

I was finishing up my final credits at Wayne County Community College before transferring to the university. The professors at Wayne County, who were mostly Black, challenged and invigorated our thinking. I felt like I belonged there. I quickly rose to the top of my class, sometimes managing the work-life balance, and sometimes tipping too far one way or the other. On several days, Taven sat in class with me, patiently playing with his Etch A Sketch or superhero toys. Sometimes, we passed a paper back and forth, silently playing Tic-Tac-Toe. I promised him ice cream on the days he was especially well-behaved.

My drive and focus made me unstoppable, my second chance at redemption clenched tightly in my hands. All my professors cheered on my determination and tenacity. They respected me as a person. I took a full load of classes, and each of those teachers embraced me in a way that I needed.

One of my Pre-Law professors was a Black lawyer. Professor Webb talked at length to me about my challenges and encouraged me to pursue my dreams. She warned me that people would perceive me in a certain way. At the time, I thought she was talking about my hair or how I dressed. But looking back, I believe she was speaking about larger issues. This professor had completed the race and I was at the starting line. She knew the stumbling blocks that I would face. Everyone wouldn't accept and embrace me as she and the other professors had done. She was telling me to be myself. That being myself has power. And that it wouldn't always be easy.

> " Everyone will not accept and embrace you; however, being yourself has power.

During those years I participated in my first literary fair, and I discovered the thrill of finding my passion. I read my writing out loud to an audience, and I felt empowered by using my words with confidence and precision. Seeing the reaction on audience members' faces sealed my desire to write and to speak. It made sense, too: all the extra-curricular activities that my parents encouraged had mostly centered around writing and poetry. At the literary fair, I felt the same energy and enthusiasm I'd felt as a child. I learned that I had a voice; I had something valuable to say, and I needed to say it.

Little did I know that the cat would have my tongue for years to come. Professor Webb was right: being myself wasn't easy. For years, the conversation lived in my head.

OUR DEEPEST FEAR

"OUR DEEPEST FEAR IS NOT THAT
WE ARE INADEQUATE.
OUR DEEPEST FEAR IS THAT
WE ARE POWERFUL BEYOND MEASURE.
IT IS OUR LIGHT, NOT OUR DARKNESS
THAT MOST FRIGHTENS US.
WE ASK OURSELVES,
'WHO AM I TO BE BRILLIANT,
GORGEOUS, TALENTED, FABULOUS?'
ACTUALLY, WHO ARE YOU NOT TO BE?
YOU ARE A CHILD OF GOD.
YOUR PLAYING SMALL
DOES NOT SERVE THE WORLD.
THERE IS NOTHING ENLIGHTENED
ABOUT SHRINKING
SO THAT OTHER PEOPLE WON'T FEEL
INSECURE AROUND YOU.
WE ARE ALL MEANT TO SHINE,
AS CHILDREN DO.
WE WERE BORN TO MAKE MANIFEST
THE GLORY OF GOD THAT IS WITHIN US.
IT'S NOT JUST IN SOME OF US;
IT'S IN EVERYONE.
AND AS WE LET OUR OWN LIGHT SHINE,
WE UNCONSCIOUSLY GIVE OTHER PEOPLE
PERMISSION TO DO THE SAME.
AS WE ARE LIBERATED FROM OUR
OWN FEAR, OUR PRESENCE
AUTOMATICALLY LIBERATES OTHERS."

MARIANNE WILLIAMSON

8

Maneuvering Racial Barriers in the Heart of Detroit

"Not everything that is faced can be changed, but nothing can be changed until it is faced."

—WESLEY BALDWIN

*M*uch of my life was spent in my car. I commuted between home and the Wayne County campus, to my various jobs, and to get my son back and forth from Muri Hill. Mom looked after Taven while I worked, and Dad sometimes kept him on the weekend. There was no way we would have survived my logistical nightmare of a life without the support of our family.

I finished at Wayne County at the top of my class, earning nearly all A's. My community college credits were exhausted, and it was time to transfer to university. I applied locally to the University of Detroit Mercy, but their decision was a letdown.

Unbelievably, the admissions committee used my ACT score from *high school* to deny my entrance. That was the very same test I'd blown off as a pregnant teen when trying to figure out my life. I don't think I spent even an hour studying for it. Yet five years later, *this* was how I was being judged. I had never experienced such a stinging rejection, but it was the first of many slammed doors in my life.

The fact that I was working full-time and maintained high grades at Wayne County while raising my son meant nothing to the decision-makers at Detroit Mercy—but their rejection made me want to get in even more. My final hope was to appeal, and then all I could do was hope.

By this point, I knew that my passion and purpose were writing and speaking publicly—the literary fairs I'd loved at Wayne County showed me that. But unfortunately, I spent years in pursuit of other things. I should have kept developing my passion. Instead, I listened to the naysayers telling me what a bad writer I was. That was a mistake. Thankfully, before I take my last breath, I'll have more opportunities to mind myself and the things that are important to me.

Although I was just in my early 20's, I felt I was already behind in life. I was seized by the fear that if I didn't make something of myself fast, I'd slide right back into being a statistic. That chip on my shoulder controlled my mind. I resented having to sell myself as "worthy enough" for Detroit Mercy. I felt like the ACT score was just an excuse, and really they didn't want another "inner city" face getting past their gated entrance. With that rejection, I internalized the messages that "you aren't smart enough," and "your scores are too low for us."

I lived to prove them wrong.

I shared all those feelings with my mother one day, while we were chatting at her kitchen table. "I can't believe I had to appeal," I complained. "It's like I haven't even started there, and they've already decided I'm not good enough."

"Nonsense," my mother sniffed. "Mileka, you're brilliant. It's their foolish mistake to reject you. It's *their* loss, not yours." Her encouragement got me through my appeal, and in August I learned I was successful. The admissions counselor didn't have much of a defense anyway. She just kept repeating that my score on a standardized test was too low, when anyone could see my ACT score was outdated.

In September, I enrolled as a junior at Detroit Mercy.

Although I'd stick out the two years, I never felt like I was a part of that school. Round One was my fight with admissions, but the battle would continue throughout my time there. Every week it seemed I was butting heads with someone, whether it was professors, the financial aid office, or arrogant students. I often wondered how things might have been different if I'd gone to Spelman. I imagine the path would have been much easier in an environment where some things could go without saying. At Detroit Mercy, I felt like I constantly needed to explain who I was and where I was from.

During my college years, I continued the process of giving myself away, even before I was confident in who I was created to be in this world. Later, I wouldn't even recognize the person I'd become. Just as they had at King Crafts, people made constant comments about my outfits, how I chose to wear my hair, and the way that I spoke. To survive in that environment, I began to shut down for fear of exploding.

Although I felt like I didn't belong at Detroit Mercy, it did challenge me intellectually. The rigor of the curriculum kept me there despite the indignities along the way. There were a few spots on campus where I found a respite. My most memorable times were in the stacks, on the top floor of the library, where all the really old books were. People rarely went up there unless they were doing a research project and needed ancient resources. I loved it. Being surrounded by nothing but wall-to-wall books was blissful. But when I exited that haven, I was met with constant signals that I was an unwelcome outsider, encouraged to hide my identity. Slowly, I disappeared.

If I could do it all again, I'd find a circle of support to deal honestly with my feelings of rejection. How many of my hang-ups were all in my mind? I was focused and determined in class, but I was not as present as I should have been with my son, my family, or even myself. My mind constantly raced through endless "to-do" tasks. I was also consumed with presenting a confident image, despite my internal conflicts. That juggling act eventually crumbled.

One Thanksgiving I was home with my family, but I'd locked myself in a separate room, trying to get some assignments done. Finishing my classwork took precedence over everything. I was determined to give it my all because I had to prove everyone wrong. According to the "majority," I wasn't supposed to be at Detroit Mercy in the first place. It was my mission to prove the naysayers wrong.

Even with my intense workload, I took on extracurricular projects and community service hours for the school. My efforts helped the school's marketing image, which was ironic. After all, Detroit was *my* community, where I'd been born and raised. And this university had built a fence around its perimeter so that people from my community would stay off its campus. As I saw it, the school's efforts to help Detroiters were tangled in limits and stipulations. It seemed that the doors of admission welcomed few sons and daughters of Detroit.

Not surprisingly, one of my favorite courses was English Literature. We read short stories by various authors from around the globe, wrote short essays, and participated in class discussions. Dr. Ida was an older white woman with a distinctive, raspy voice, and her questions made me think about other people's perspectives.

In Dr. Ida's class, I learned about indigenous people. I learned about European people. I read about things that were familiar to me, such as "passing." Not passing my classes, which I was focused on, but the thing that "light-skinned" Black people did post-slavery in order to enjoy "white privilege." We discussed the intricacies of such a decision, such as when a "passing" woman married a white man and got pregnant. Her pregnancy would then be an agony of anxiety, as she feared having a baby who couldn't "pass." I was familiar with this topic, as I and many other Americans have fair-skinned family members who still pass as white Americans.

After an enjoyable two months in Dr. Ida's class, it was time for mid-semester reviews. Dr. Ida walked down the center aisle of the classroom, handing out our midterm grades. I knew my overall score because my folder full of graded papers was all A's—but her grade book told a different story. She had marked me down with zeros for the entire semester. I was present daily in the first seat facing her lectern, yet she'd given me a slate of zeros. *Are you kidding me?* I had perfect attendance and was enthusiastic about the class discussions—but I was FAILING.

After class, I asked to see her grade book to compare it with my graded assignments. One after the next, she called out the assignment and my grade.

"Zero," Dr. Ida read out.

"No, Professor, that's an A." Over and over again we did this. A semester's worth of hard work, nearly 15 assignments, were marked as ZERO in her book. Before that little exercise was over, I said, "Look at the scores on the line below mine."

The student below me had all my grades on his assignments. I knew who he was, too. This guy rarely came to class and clearly didn't turn in any homework. The professor had awarded him my A's and chastised me with his zeros.

Dr. Ida agreed to change my grades since I'd shown her the proof. She said she'd let the other guy "keep" the grades in the book—*my* grades, that is.

Being the fearless junior I was, I asked her to think about why she would make a mistake like that. Had she done it consciously? How could she confuse me with a student who never came to class or turned in assignments, when here I was, sitting right in front of her? Could it be about race?

Dr. Ida was floored as the advocacy boiled up in me. We left that day a bit uneasy—but at least we had a corrected grade book.

Later that semester, Dr. Ida called me into her office to talk about the grade book conversation. "I was surprised when you said that Mileka," she admitted. "Actually I was shocked. And for a while, I felt quite cross with you. Nothing like that has ever happened to me before, and I've been teaching for thirty-five years now. But in retrospect, I think you may have been right. I'm sorry. I just don't think I saw you as an A student."

Wow, she was honest. I was proud of my courage. I'd stood up for myself and challenged her motives. As to that white classmate who barely came to class, she'd given him a string of unearned A's. Just because of who he was and how he looked, he had a leg up on me from the start. No matter how hard I worked, I knew I would never be seen as enough in a predominately white learning environment.

I hid my anger, though. "Thank you, Dr. Ida," I told her. "I really do appreciate your taking my words to heart." But on the inside, my mind was blown.

This was a woman who I admired, someone who taught me about understanding different perspectives from around the world. Yet her reality was something quite different. That day, I felt a little hatred for the white guy who never came to class, and that seed of resentment kept growing until it gripped me in law school. Even in his absence, Dr. Ida had seen him—or at least, she'd imagined she did. I sat front and center consistently, and still, I was invisible to her.

That wasn't the last of my misfortunes at Detroit Mercy. I was the first to sign up for a new class called "The Black Body." I felt sure this course would explore the pains of my people and walk us through a bit of the history and triumph that my ancestors had experienced in America. But in the end, that class left me more traumatized than Dr. Ida's grade book experience.

Instead of reviewing Black people's experience in American history from a positive stance, the entire curriculum was negative. There were about 20 of us in the class, two-thirds were Black, and the others were white. Two of the white students had opinions on everything.

There is a danger in allowing outsiders to narrate the experiences and perspectives of an entire group of people. Especially when those opinions are ill-informed. Unfortunately, Professor Dillard mostly agreed with the white students' viewpoints, never really setting the record straight when they asserted themselves as superior humans—despite his reddish-brown skin and mid-back dreadlocks.

> " There is a danger in allowing outsiders to narrate the experiences and perspectives of an entire group of people. Especially when those opinions are ill-informed.

One day, in a discussion about Black hair, the two white blabbermouths really crossed the line. "It's obvious why they straighten it," one boy declared. "Kinky hair is looked down on in our society."

"Yeah," a white girl agreed. "It's like, subconsciously? They want to be white."

Excuse me?! No sir and no ma'am! Try again.

One by one, each of the Black women in the class corrected them. "The way that we wear our hair does *not*—at least for me as a Black woman—in no way, shape, or form mean that I want to look white," I informed them.

The white girl looked bored. "Really? Then why *do* you straighten your hair?"

I couldn't believe her ignorance. "Hairstyles are an expression of our *individuality*. Do you think if I wore my hair in an Afro puff, that would necessarily mean that I want to join the Black Panthers?"

"We can be versatile, you know," another Black classmate cut in. "In all ways, even our hairstyles. That doesn't mean we lack self-love."

"And it *sure* doesn't mean we want to be *white*,"I concurred.

"All right Mileka," the professor held his hand up. "I think you may be taking this a little too personally."

But how could I not? Here I was attending school in the middle of a Black neighborhood, and I felt attacked for the color of my skin. Despite the location of our campus, Detroit Mercy was filled with white people who had limited exposure to Black people. Now, these same kids were telling me I wanted to be white. That was too far and too much to endure. I couldn't sit quietly any longer.

After class, the other Black students rallied around and talked about how we felt. Finally, we'd defended ourselves in a long overdue way. It was our exhale moment.

I shook that experience off, as I did countless others. And I know I wasn't the only local student who felt frustrated and excluded. To this day, it still baffles me how my college did not reflect the surrounding community. Elementary, middle, and high schools in Detroit are filled with Black students, but in Detroit universities, faces like mine are rare.

Deep inside, I couldn't help but wonder if that setup was intentional. One day in senior year, a girl named Toni told me she was in jeopardy of not graduating from her engineering program because her professor refused to speak with her. She was the only Black person in her major. Sitting outside the Liberal Arts building, she resisted tears as she racked her brain for ways to catch his attention.

She'd set up meetings with him which he'd neglected to attend. He wouldn't see her during his office hours and refused to talk to her in class. I consoled Toni that day, but her story gave me one more reason to feel like an unwelcome black sheep in a mostly white college.

Then, as always, there were money problems. I felt like the world was telling me to quit. When I could no longer meet my tuition payment, I applied for state assistance. Do you know what I had to do, to qualify for cash assistance? The state of Michigan required all applicants to actively seek employment from 9 am to 5 pm *daily*. How was I supposed to go to school and also spend all day in front of a computer, applying for jobs?

I went into the state welfare office to discuss my options, and there I sat face-to-face with a buttoned-up woman whose name tag said "Monique."

"The solution is easy," she told me as she straightened some papers on her desk. "You just need to meet the job search requirements."

Was she deaf? *I just told you, I attend Detroit Mercy full-time.*

Monique and I faced off with one another across her tiny desk. The room had about ten other workers in it, all meeting with applicants for benefits. There was no privacy to discuss my poor financial situation. I'm sure the other applicants felt just as embarrassed as I did when talking to a complete stranger about being broke and needing help with life's basic needs like shelter and food–all in a room full of listening strangers. It was degrading and humiliating.

What I wanted to do was spitfire. Instead, I pleaded for an exception.

"Ms. Monique, there must be some other solution that does not involve me dropping out of school." She didn't say anything, so I kept going. "I'm almost done with college; I only have a semester to go. I can't just drop out now. What would that show my son?"

She still didn't say anything, but she leaned in a little closer. Was that compassion I saw in her eyes? "I've taken care of us up until this point, and I only need a little time before graduating. In just a few months, I'll have my bachelor's degree and I can earn more money."

Monique let out a deep sigh, as though I were asking her for the world on a platter. "Okay, okay, Mileka. We can make an exception for you to attend your classes." She went to her desk and pulled out a single sheet of paper. "Have each of your professors sign and verify your coursework and bring it back to the office no later than next Wednesday."

This lady is bonkers, I thought. What would my professors think of me? They all had their lives together, and here I was, applying for welfare. *Just another statistic,* I thought, as my eyes started to blur with tears. "Is there any other way?" I asked. "Could I, like, bring you my transcripts?"

"No," she said flatly, her eyes flicking back to her paperwork. "We need the signatures."

A few days passed before I had the courage to ask each of my six professors to sign off.

I sat in my classes, my mind consumed with doubts. *How are they going to perceive me now? Maybe I really don't belong here. I bet no other student has to do this type of thing to preserve their seat in school.*

But one by one, after each class, the professors signed that form without questions. Relief flooded me with each signature. The heaviness and fear of being kicked out of school slowly lifted off my shoulders, but the shame and embarrassment lingered.

The final humiliation came a week later when I was called in to see Darby, the financial aid advisor. She'd never been friendly towards me, and one day, she saw an opportunity to unleash her abuse.

My appointment was for 1:15, but it was after two when she opened the door. "Mileka?" she called, looking past me into the empty hallway.

I got up from my chair and followed her as she lumbered back into her office. "You have an outstanding bill that needs to be paid," she announced, squeezing between the desk and her seat.

"I know," I admitted. "I lost my job recently, and I've been working odd jobs to cover the bills. I applied for state assistance, as well—"

At that, I could have sworn I saw her smile. Was it *funny* to her that I'd applied for state assistance?

"So I only have $350 to pay today," I fumbled, taking out my checkbook, "but if there's any way you could help me find scholarships or grants to finance the balance—"

That's when she cut me off, settling back in her chair. "That won't be possible today as we require the full amount," she smiled grimly, revealing a mouthful of nicotine-stained teeth. "Have you considered, Ms. Jonson, if you cannot afford the tuition payments, you probably don't belong here?"

Wait—*what*?

This lady was verbalizing exactly what the institution had signaled to me from the beginning: "Mileka, you don't belong here." All I could think was: *I am* this *close to the finish line, with a handful of credits left to complete, and I* still *don't belong here.* But this native Detroiter deserved to fight for her seat. I laced up my boxing gloves, got in the ring, and punched right back.

"You know what?" I told Darby, my voice shaking with tears. "If your best solution is to advise an honor student who's a few credits away from graduating to drop out, then fine. Just put that in writing so I can address your decision with the head of financial aid, and maybe the Dean while I'm at it." Then I stood up. "I'll pay what I can today. And I'll pay the rest—well, I'll pay it just as soon as I can."

And with that, I walked out.

And you know what happened? That same day she found more scholarships I qualified for, and that's how I paid for that semester.

Despite my many obstacles at Detroit Mercy, I came out on the other side as a better person. Despite Dr. Ida doubting my abilities, and despite Darby encouraging me to drop out, I rose to the top of my class. On graduation day, people's opinions and perceptions of me didn't matter. That day was mine. The piece of paper that I was given on graduation day carried with it all the experiences that had once been barriers to me. Each barrier was an opportunity to fight for my goals. My advocacy skills were being built for my future, just as my skin was thickening for the tougher experiences ahead.

> **"** I was caught up in the idea that I was someone because of something I'd accomplished. I thought my value was in my work, and not in the essence of being human.

From the stands in the Titan gym, I could hear my family's voices cheering for me. Mom's distinct whistle filled me with pride. That same whistle that I'd dreaded hearing when she called for my siblings and me to come home had become a signal that my tribe was present. My entire family was there to support me: my parents, my siblings, my son, and my grandfather Poppy. All of them were rooting for me as we all had conquered my goal together.

It was my love of learning that kept me in school. The resentment I felt for not fitting in gave me the fuel to move quickly toward my degree. I stayed focused enough to graduate *magna cum laude,* but I felt that my personal growth had regressed. At Detroit Mercy, I wasn't the same confident student that I'd been at Wayne County.

Degree in hand, I felt sure I was well on my way to success, and no more being broke. I might not have been the same zealous student I'd been at Wayne County, but I was *somebody*—a first-generation college graduate.

Now I know that was false. I was caught up in the idea that I was someone because of something I'd accomplished. I thought my value was in my work, and not in the essence of being human. That degree made me hold my head both higher and lower, simultaneously. Some things were going right...but more important things were fading.

9

Thickening Grind

"A woman is like a tea bag; you never know how strong she is until she gets in hot water."

—ELEANOR ROOSEVELT

A degree in English holds limited possibilities for a bronze-skinned, complex young lady like me. And once I graduated, I wasn't even sure where to begin looking for a smart career path. Maybe there had been career counselors at Detroit Mercy, but I'd never met them. I was just focused on getting through school. Naively, I thought economic stability would automatically follow.

It didn't. Eventually, I stumbled my way into a paralegal job—right back to where I'd been before school.

One of my first job interviews was menacing. I was interviewed by the entire compliance department at Clayton International simultaneously—a panel of ten people, mostly white, mostly lawyers. Everyone was much older than I was, but somehow, I held my ground. Before I made it to the car, they called me to offer me the job. Fresh out of college, and I was already on my way!

Then, three days after I started my new job, a single phone call changed my life.

By that time, Antony and I had separated. The demands and expectations we had for each other had been far too unrealistic. Now we had a rocky co-parenting relationship, and we certainly didn't talk every day. So I was surprised when my phone rang and it was Farrah, Antony's mother. When I picked up the call, she was sobbing so hard she couldn't speak. Eventually, she formed enough words to express what no mother should ever have to say. Her son, the pride and joy of her life, was dead.

At the tender age of 28, Antony had given all that he ever would to our ten-year-old son. Taven would not have his father to cheer him at his baseball games or chess tournaments. Antony would miss the newspaper article featuring Taven and his natural golfing talent. The father-son relationship that many take for granted was a gift my son would never enjoy. He was left with just faint memories and passing moments from his short ten years with Antony.

I felt ill-equipped to raise a child alone, and I had no idea how to console my son in the emptiness of his mourning. The moment when I gave Taven the news slapped the bright smile off my little child's face in an instant. Now, at ten years old, he bore a heaviness that not even I had experienced: the loss of a parent. What was a young mother to do to comfort her child who did not shed a tear? Overnight, Taven had to be the man of the house. He had to fill the shoes of a grown man without his first male teacher.

Taven's first experience with death was his own father. Between Farrah and Taven, the pain was enough to last a lifetime. For me, the greatest agony was knowing there was nothing that I, as a mother, could do to stop my child from hurting. I felt so helpless. I knew that nothing I said or did would make my son understand why he would never see his daddy again.

Here I was trying to make a better life. I was finally healing the wounds of my teenage mom trauma. I had barely stepped one foot into my new life when my entire world shattered. I blindly raced to pick up the pieces so my son would not feel the cuts of his father's premature death.

Antony's gone-too-soon story is all too familiar. His death was one of youth and hubris, one whose details I will reserve out of my love for Taven and my respect for his privacy. Should he ever wish to share that story, I will allow time and space for him to do so.

I do know this: Antony's death impelled me on my mad race to become a super parent.

I lost any zeal for Clayton because for me it symbolized a bookmark in a life stained with the blood of Antony's passing. Perhaps that's why I stayed at Clayton for as long as I did, despite the fact that the work was a long series of mundane bean-counting tasks.

For every year that Taven had known Antony, I spent in misery at work.

Ten years of answering calls, opening envelopes, and responding to letters were mind-numbing and endless. But at the same time, four years of higher education served me well. Learning the ins and outs of compliance and handling Board communications was a long, time-consuming process—but I'm a quick study, and despite my grief, I shone.

At Clayton International, I was part of a company made up of "successful people." Most of them were married, had families, and had graduated from top universities. They were paid well and seemed to have it all together, living the American Dream. Most of their homes were located in affluent communities, at least half an hour outside of Detroit.

Now I wanted their successful status for Taven. He, at *least*, deserved that stability. I wanted to cross over from being the one who *supported* the attorneys, to actually *being* one.

But then my insecurities took over. I was kidding myself with those lofty professional ambitions. My resentment towards Antony grew for not doing his share with our son and for preventing us from having the life that these "successful people" enjoyed—and the one I'd known as a child.

Bent on defying the "she's a single mom" label, I kept my head down and tried to learn the environment. But the goal post kept moving. Each day when I looked in the mirror, the person looking back at me was a lost, unhappy stranger who was failing as a mother. A foreigner, stuck in a melancholic workplace, feeling isolated and alone.

When I first started working at Clayton International, I defended myself on a regular basis. Some of my courage came from the fury I felt from Antony's death. That fire fizzled, and then I became numb to the microaggressions. I began to excuse injurious behavior, most of which was subtle unfairness. I let comments go by without challenge. Who had I become? I learned that subtle prejudice can rear its ugly head when people talk about certain geographic locations. "Detroit" was a buzzword for Black. They were calling it a "jungle," a "war zone," and dissing Black family units, laughing about how few years there were between the generations, and what that said about teenage motherhood. The point of all those jokes was to assert their superiority.

I no longer knew how to defend myself the way I had on my first day of kindergarten. I sank deeper and deeper into a self-pity that bloomed into doubt. Some days were so bad that I cried outside in my car before going in to work. My emotional swings went undetected because I avoided personal conversations. My coworkers and I didn't feel comfortable sharing our lives with one another; likely because we had little in common. We lived different lives. I silently observed their world, and they jumped at the chance to judge mine.

> **Introspection became my means of survival after the dust settled from the culture shock.**

My white colleagues were comfortable mocking Detroiters, even with me there in front of them. I felt stuck. If I said what was truly on my mind, I'd quickly be labeled an "angry Black woman." Besides, they were all older lawyers whose emotional pulse was different than mine. There were too many wrong opinions for me to correct. How could my words matter?

Being around those people, especially after my undergraduate experience in a predominately white environment, gave me a different perspective. Introspection became my means of survival after the dust settled from the culture shock.

People talk about "fight or flight"—but my flight was inward. Keeping quiet allowed me to stay in that environment, support my family, and pursue my dreams. I'd master the job and keep it in perspective. My co-workers were not my friends.

We were there to work. This would not be my end, working in a tense environment, giving myself and most of my time to a company whose people didn't want me there.

Maybe they were able to check a corporate responsibility box by keeping a black female "token" there. It could be that their intentions weren't bad. They had few experiences with Black people. I let the opportunities to clear up misconceptions slip past me because it was too exhausting being the spokesperson for every person who bore a skin tone similar to mine. As I concentrated on creating a better lifestyle for Taven and me, I longed for a magic wand that would wipe Taven's agony from his little face.

My focus on creating a better life kept me grounded. Law school was my magic carpet ride—or so I thought.

10

Jump In

"Life is either a daring adventure or
nothing at all."

– HELLEN KELLER

*A*fter a pile of law school rejections, I finally got a YES from the very same place where I did my undergraduate: Detroit Mercy. I was prepared to go full-time, but my job at Clayton International was surprisingly supportive. They agreed to let me keep my job while I pursued my dream.

I planned to keep working full-time and take evening classes. It was the only way to climb up from the bottom tier of society's hierarchy. Once I became a lawyer, I was convinced that people would change their perception of me. I would think better of myself too.

I believed that by learning the systems that govern every aspect of our lives, I would magically undo the psychological hatred I felt toward myself. To me, pursuing the law was the only solution. *If I change, then I'll be better.* My better self would achieve my vision of success.

The next five years for me were all work and no play. Little did I know my mental well-being was hanging in the balance.

Just as at Detroit Mercy undergrad, there were few local students at Detroit Mercy Law School. In fact, I believe the school enrolls more Canadian students than native Detroiters. Maybe five or six students in my class looked like me. Nonetheless, my classmates were relatable—mainly because we all worked during the day. Most of us attended night school because we all had grown-up responsibilities.

Classes were held four nights a week, from 6pm to 10 pm, after a full day of work. And like most law schools, Detroit Mercy used the Socratic method to explain legal doctrine. Oh, the agony! Every cell in my body dreaded being called

91

on to recite the facts, issues, or law in any one of several cases we were assigned in our relentless reading assignments.

Mr. Mazurek, our Contracts professor, especially enjoyed torturing us. It amused him to ask question after question, without ever revealing if our answers were right or wrong. The probing questions were endless, and in the end, he would yell, "You've been Mazurek'd!"

He let us know who had the superior intellect in the room. Between Contracts class, my other grueling courses, and working as a legal assistant, I was growing a layer of thick skin that protected my budding insecurities from the outside world.

Both at school and the office, I was in survival-and-fight mode. And since I was a first-generation lawyer, I didn't know who to turn to when I was drowning. I managed the culture shock at work but fell short of connecting with other attorneys, so I concealed my weakness. And most of them weren't interested in showing me the ropes.

Clarissa was one colleague who surprised me. She asked me about law school, and when I told her about my hellacious Contracts class, she actually offered to help. That day after work, I followed her home to borrow her Contracts notes from her law school days. I trailed behind her in my Crown Vicky for 15 minutes. We cut through streets that I'd always passed, with beautiful houses and carefully manicured lawns.

When we got to her house, I parked on the street as she pulled into her driveway.

"MOMMY!" Her rambunctious children bolted into her arms. She hugged them tightly as she waved for me to join her, and we walked up the steps of her porch to her front door.

I stood in the foyer, admiring the open space and high ceilings. Watching her kids howl and prance around the living room, my mind drifted to my even-tempered, well-behaved son. I was lucky my kid wasn't so loud...wasn't I? *Or are these kids so boisterous because they feel safe?* Maybe if I were home more often, Taven would feel brave enough to misbehave occasionally.

Clarissa returned with a binder labeled "Contracts" in her hands. I thanked her profusely, and she ushered me out the front door with a slight smile. Clarissa had made her contribution to my lawyer journey.

Before I made it off the porch, the door closed. Back in Crown Vicky, I laid the binder in the passenger seat and reversed my mixtape to sing along with Goapele's "Closer to My Dreams." Excited that I finally had a clue about my puzzling Contracts class, I opened the binder and began reading the material. All those flow charts and acronyms— with a sinking heart, I realized it was impenetrable.

Trying to decipher Clarissa's 15-year-old notes was just too time-consuming, and after a couple of frustrated evenings, I put her binder to the side.

A few days later, she asked if the material had been helpful. "Yes, it's much clearer than the class," I lied. What was I supposed to do? I couldn't admit to her that I needed more than just another set of notes to read. I needed someone to talk me through some of the principles in the text to help me grasp them. That wasn't going to happen. She was too busy and we weren't that close. The real mistake I made was in expecting her, or anyone at the job, to jump in and save my sinking ship.

Although my co-workers acted as if they supported me, their subtle comments said otherwise. My gut said they wanted me to know my place and stay there. Consequently, I worried about everything. The way I styled my hair, how I spoke, what I wore, the color of my nails, how my son looked, how he dressed, and where I graduated high school. I listened to my colleagues chatter about their children's schools, or their own private high schools and colleges. They had things in common, a basis for small talk. Their world was foreign, and I had no passport to get there.

My co-workers knew little about my world, but that didn't stop them from voicing their disdain for Detroit and its people. One day, Clarissa and I were driving toward the municipal court through a blighted area of Detroit that had once thrived.

"I don't know how anyone can live like this," she commented, shaking her head in judgment.

What a snub, I thought, sitting in the back passenger seat of her company-paid-for luxury SUV. That afternoon, we drove to a restaurant in southwest Detroit. Instead of taking the freeway, she chose to drive the slower, scenic route.

"*This* area doesn't seem safe," she observed, clicking the automatic door locks.

I fumed, speechless.

The indignities continued in law school. Each year, first-year law students participated in moot court. Some of us knew our target and went after it vigorously. Some were uncertain, and others puked at the pressure, literally.

I had a command of my material and was sure of my points. I practiced my arguments and rebuttal in the mirror over and over again. "May it please the Court," I repeated to my own reflection. Finally, the day of the competition arrived.

I strode into the classroom with complete confidence that my arguments would prevail, though my hopes of taking first place were low. I knew the probability of a Black student winning the competition was limited. It was more of a "check the box" exercise for me.

The entire first-year class gathered in the tall ceiling atrium, all dressed in business attire. Students were paired off and told where to go before the judges. My opponent was a full-time day student. He was Asian. I extended my hand just before we started our arguments. He rocked back and forth in his chair, biting the nails on his left hand while he shook my hand with his right.

My opponent argued for the plaintiff, and I did the defense. The substance of what we were arguing about escapes me to this day, but I remember the judges staring at their notepads and grading scales.

Finally, they handed down their assessments. At first, their comments went as expected: my arguments were persuasive and clear, and my rebuttal was on point. But then one judge, a woman, lifted her hand to interject.

"You were too loud," she remarked.

Say what? How do I respond to that? I'm a passionate speaker. Isn't that a desirable trait in litigation? That judge made me feel like I'd been screaming. It was an unintelligent comment to me; anyway, volume was not what we would be scored on. Once again, it felt like the target was shifting to keep me in my place.

Keeping true to who I was, I thanked the judges and withheld my fury. I collected my papers from the podium, but I'm sure my facial expression exposed my true feelings.

Later that day, I learned that one of my friends had made the quarterfinals. Camille was an incredible Black woman. She argued intelligently and poignantly, and we'd all been impressed with her performance. But her opponent was a blue-eyed white guy in his early 20s. He got a higher score.

In the case of Camille, her criticism was that she was too "soft-spoken." And it was the same judge! That's right; the same woman who told me I was too loud told Camille she needed to speak up.

How was it constructive to tell us we were too loud or too soft-spoken? It would have been far more impactful to say, "Be mindful of the inflections and tone of your voice to capture your audience." I'd been anticipating a critique of my argument. Heck, even a lesson in public speaking would have sufficed. I would have enjoyed some guidance on how to address a jury or judge when arguing a motion, which would have helped my development. Telling me I was too loud did nothing for my growth. It just made me shut down even more.

Witnessing my friend being told she was too quiet was infuriating. I'd been sitting in the back of the room when I heard her arguments. Both competitors were loud enough to hear easily. Neither was noticeably louder than the other. So, when the judge came in with another volume critique, I knew the competition was rigged.

When I heard Camille's assessment, I grabbed my tote and stormed out of the classroom. The only thing stopping me from leaving school right away was the responsibility I felt to congratulate and console my friend. Five minutes later, she came out of the classroom, and a few of us cheered her on for advancing to the quarterfinals. We all thought she'd been treated unfairly, but Camille was too optimistic to dwell on it. So we bit our tongues and left, still feeling a tingle of disappointment.

> " Once the job has first begun, never leave it until it is done. Be the labor great or small; do it well or not at all.

That day, I decided that I'd stop pounding my head against a brick wall in a world that didn't want me there. Law school was the "ticket," but it was starting to feel like a coupon to nowhere. At the same time, quitting was not an option. My grandmother Grace taught me, "*Once the job has first begun, never leave it until it is done. Be the labor great or small; do it well or not at all.*" And so I attempted to do it all: work, school, and parenting. I'd never gotten the home part down; I lived in chaos. By default, my son was raised in anarchy.

My home life might have been chaotic, but I turned up to work every day in the correct professional attire. My originality was gone. Barely getting by, I mimicked what I saw to fit in. If I could adapt to the corporate world, I believed, then success for me was certain. That distorted line of thinking got me nowhere.

Suffocating in the rarified world that I chose to be in caused me to lose focus on the things that were important, like my family, my son, and even my own well-being. I had to prove to myself that I was not a failure, no longer the pregnant teenager who had "ruined" her life. This lawyer thing *had* to work out for me. I was beyond exhaustion, my personality and spirit eroding—but I kept pressing.

I knew I had changed since attending Wayne County. The student I'd been in my early *20*s readily volunteered to place herself in front of any crowd. She was alive! Her eyes were set on doing whatever she could to change the entire world. That Mileka led without a second thought. She was confident. She wanted to make the world a better place *and* appreciate the small things, and she was vividly present at the moment.

Now, a first-year law student, I was stale, stiff, and afraid. Most disappointing was that I feared being me. I was a stretched, cracking, rubber band ball of nerves—about to snap.

Then I made my situation even worse. Not taking time to consider the anguish that I was piling on, I joined every organization I could in my attempt to connect to law school. You name it, and I was either a member or in the ranks of student leadership. I joined the State Bar of Michigan's law student section, the American Bar Association's law student section, and President the Black Law Students Association (BLSA). I interned at law firms and state and federal courts. I was a Voice for Justice Fellow at a local non-profit. I was doing the most, more than any sane person could possibly expect.

In each of those new ventures, I was searching for zeal. I longed for the bond of being fully connected to the institutions where I was spending most of my life. I deserved that, right? But despite my best efforts, I didn't believe that I belonged in those places myself. Quite the opposite. Instead, I bought into the negative things I thought others believed about me.

With every move I made, I worried that I was wrong or could have done things better. Constantly afraid that someone, anyone, would see my flaws, I faded into the background of my own world. Not feeling as though I could share my insecurities with anyone, I kept my feelings of being a misfit to myself.

In retrospect, I cheated myself out of the full experience of law school. There was little enjoyment in my life. Taven was a budding teenager at that point, so he and I didn't always see eye-to-eye. When he started high school, he came up to my nose, but by his sophomore year, he was towering over me. Between 13 and 15, he went through a major transition. Overnight he started putting meticulous effort into grooming himself, taking hour-long showers. His round face thinned into an oval shape like mine, his black mustache peeping through his silky brown skin. Taven had always been kind-hearted, and I know he quietly suffered from my absence. All I did was work, school, and study. And our family time, when we had it, was usually in the middle of the night.

Each night after class, I hit the John C. Lodge Freeway straight to my parents' house. I got there at a quarter to 11 pm, religiously. A sensible person would dash, grab her child, and go. Not me. I had to level up some normalcy. My son, mother, and father took turns welcoming me back to safety. I greeted everyone in the house, made myself a plate, and ate dinner at the kitchen table. Taven would then tell me a little about his life, usually while chatting with friends on the phone or in front of the television. Mom sat with me at the table to hear me rant about my day. She was my closest confidante, lending an ear every night to help heal the mental bruising I'd endured that day.

While I stuffed my face, she sat there in her pajamas, just listening. Eating helped me calm down, and then my exhaustion kicked in. We watched reruns of our favorite soap operas, and in the wee hours of the morning, I'd finally fall dead asleep.

Toward the end of my law school curriculum, I had a lapse of sanity. With nearly a semester to go, I decided that a JD was not enough. It was too ordinary. One day in class, I saw a pamphlet advertising a dual JD-MBA program in the atrium.

Astoundingly, I didn't run the other way. Instead, I thought, *You've always wanted your MBA. It's now or never.*

The next morning, I called the business school to inquire about admissions, and with my credentials, I was accepted on the spot. I was excited, but before the business school could enroll me, the law school had to sign off—and that was a problem.

Professor Krumpy, the law school coordinator for the JD-MBA program, never seemed to answer his phone. His voicemail always picked up. I emailed. No response. Finally, after several dozen calls, he agreed to meet with me.

The day we were scheduled to meet, I was ill but had a full day of work and classes. Killing time before my meeting, I got to chat with some students about BLSA. As I recall, the two candidates who were running for president of BLSA were not that friendly toward each other, and that bothered me. It wasn't good for the organization, and I felt strongly that the Black student population needed to be unified.

Then from nowhere, I blurted, "I think I'll run for president myself." *Where did that come from?* Already feverish, I felt instantly sicker. And then, it was time for my meeting.

I headed upstairs to meet with Dr. Krumpy. And no sooner had I sat in his office than he pronounced his verdict.

"You need to focus on getting your JD," he told me.

Here we go.

He cleared his throat officiously. "You have about a year left, and I don't think it's good to start the MBA program right now."

I felt my fury rising. We hadn't discussed anything. He didn't even ask what I had to say before he made up an opinion about my life. We'd never even officially met before, yet he was adamant that my goals were too hefty: I should aim lower.

Calming my frustration, I asked, "Dr. Krumpy, why do you think I should wait?"

"You're too far along in the JD program," he explained, glancing at some notes on his desk. "And it says here you scored low in your Property class."

"That's true," I conceded, "but it's also true that I'm working full-time while going to school. This is now or never, Dr. Krumpy. I need to get on with my life once I graduate."

We went round and round and ended nowhere. He insisted that I focus on my JD, and I was determined to pursue the MBA program. And the more he told me "no," the more adamant I became.

After the disastrous meeting in Dr. Krumpy's office, my friends at BLSA helped me to devise a plan. First, I went to my Property professor. She agreed to write a recommendation letter, including in it the caveat that my "grade in her class was not a testament to my intellect." She saw me and believed in me, even in my darkest moments of invisibility.

Her letter helped, but Dr. Krumpy still dragged his feet. I hounded him, sending note after note, until nearly a semester later, he finally sent the second part of my acceptance, accompanied by a long letter detailing his opinion on how I should *not* go forward with the dual program.

Without a rational explanation for his concerns, I had to conclude that his doubts stemmed from the fact that I was Black. He never said it, and it never came up.

It was impossible to get through the dual degree program and raise my son while working—but I did it. I'm not sure how, but I did. When I was in the thick of it, I just moved through my work, never giving a thought to my constant fatigue and mind fog. The path was clear, and I was nearly at the finish line. *I have to finish,* I told myself. *Quitting is not an option. What would that show my son? That when things get tough, you bow out?*

> **66** Quitting is not an option!

No, quitting was not in my character. It was against what my grandmother Grace had taught me. And so my world was in constant disarray, living day-by-day without the order that I needed and without Godly structure for myself or my son. Now I realize the impact that onerous schedule had on me, and I can only imagine how my son must have felt during my decade-long school journey.

I was a robot. Only striving for success, I believed, would get me out of the realm of being a negative statistic. That concept was ingrained in my head. *Push harder.* This is what was required of me, as a Black woman and a "non-traditional student."

Each semester, my chest filled with guilt for not being present for my son, my family, or myself. I'm sure that Taven got frustrated with me being gone so much. Even when he did see me, I usually had my nose pressed in a book. But getting through this, I thought, would make everything perfect for us all.

Taven's childhood was difficult. No one was around to help with his homework or take the time to debrief him about his day. My son had to experience the pains of high school by himself. I felt like a negligent parent at times. Sometimes, I admit that my patience was thin, and I unfairly ridiculed him for trivial things. My stress levels were off the charts. So were his, probably.

We talked, but our relationship could have been closer if I'd had just a little bit more time for him. Once, when he was 16, I recall snapping at him and apologizing. I was horrified, but being the kind-hearted person that he is, Taven said that it was okay and that he understood.

"How do you understand stress?" I demanded. "Kids don't get stressed."

Taven gave me a look. "Yes, kids do. We have all kinds of stress."

"Like what?"

He ticked off all his worries on his fingers. "Like school, friends, social life, social media, trying to figure things out for the future—believe me, Mom, we have stress."

Duh. Of course, my son was having all sorts of challenges that I couldn't help him with, mainly because I was absent, chasing the hour hand to our "better life."

Before I started law school, I'd been vigilant about fellowshipping with God. When I was in the thick of it, I let my faith slip—and that's the thing I regret the most. I started with the misconception that "I can do it all." The truth is, I was doing what *I* wanted. And because I felt like I had to try harder than my counterparts, I sold myself short in so many ways.

11

Revving up for the Bar Exam, Take 1

"Whether you think you can or you think
you can't, you're right."

—HENRY FORD

*I*n December 2013, I checked several triumphant boxes. Finish law school, check. Complete graduate business school, check. Celebrate Taven's eighteenth birthday, check!

I was DONE. The laborious work of law school was behind me, and I even managed to earn a second degree along the way! Now it was bye-bye to the endless syllabi. Ten years after getting my bachelor's degree, I collected two more precious pieces of paper. I won.

This should have been a time for celebrating my victories, but my mission still felt incomplete. The February 2014 bar exam loomed over my head, so there was no time to commemorate my past five years of drudgery. My family and I celebrated my son's birthday with dinner. His milestone to manhood deserved more than dinner at a restaurant, but I was too preoccupied with my goals to plan anything more.

Taven's needs didn't conform to my accelerated test prep. He needed me to help him prepare for his senior trip to Europe, which was right around exam day. We had to schedule passport pictures, fill out his passport application, complete forms for his school, and attend school meetings to discuss the trip. My attention was constantly divided, and for once it seemed to irritate him. He kept having to remind me about discussions we'd had only recently. Occasionally, he'd grumble, "Mom, you just asked me that," or "We talked about that yesterday, you don't remember?" Here he was, about to take off for his first trip abroad, and I wasn't showing much excitement about what he was doing—I was distracted by my own timeline.

Before crossing the stage with my law degree, I planned to have my bar license—which gave me just three months to study. I severely underestimated the amount of time, energy, and focus needed to get there. Why was I pushing so hard, anyway? I forged full speed ahead, doubting myself every minute, constantly worried that others were judging me.

After completing my classwork, I didn't even take a moment to breathe. I was determined to push-push-push and get the test behind me. That familiar nagging feeling of incompleteness haunted me, so I hurried forward, thinking I was getting a head start. Burned out as I was, I was foolish to think clicking my heels and forcing my nose into yet another book would get me anywhere. But by that time, my negative self-talk was in high gear. I exhausted all my energy discouraging myself from within.

> " I forged full speed ahead, doubting myself every minute, constantly worried that others were judging me.

The angst and anticipation of sitting for the bar began to eat away at me. I was unraveling, and no one knew. Telling everyone that I was taking the exam in February kept them all away from me, and that was how I wanted it.

I acted like I had a plan. During my last semester in law school, I met with several people to get their advice. I thought if I collected enough "nuggets of wisdom," I would have enough knowledge to magically get a passing score. My lunch breaks were set aside for attorney meetings. I carefully jotted down each piece of advice as if it were a gold coin I could keep in my pocket. I should have spent some of those hours honing my study skills, instead of taking meticulous notes on what worked for others.

One discussion with a former professor scared me. More than anyone else, she was brutally honest about the time and commitment it took to pass the bar. There weren't any tricks or shortcuts, she cautioned—I would need to master the material and become one with it. "Know the law, cold!" she commanded.

Now I know her advice was solid. But back then, I was too stuck in my own head to listen.

By then, I knew I had some challenges to overcome with the linear, logical thinking that was necessary for the law. When I spoke up in class, I never gave myself enough time to think through my ideas before saying them out loud. Professor Felder called it my "spider web thinking," and some of my classmates echoed his opinion.

You know the confused look people give you after you speak when you've failed to make yourself clear? That look happened to me too often, and it messed with my confidence.

I also had a hard time concentrating on my studies. My plan was to kick off bar prep by listening to every Kaplan study CD—about 50-plus hours' worth of material. Don't get me wrong, I studied for weeks, but my mind just wasn't focused enough. The problem was that listening to someone else discuss a legal concept didn't mean I understood it, and it certainly didn't mean I could pass a test on the subject. But as long as I was listening to those recordings, I told myself I was doing everything I could to pass.

When people asked how my studies were going, I put a big, bright, plastic smile on my face. "I plan to listen to all the recordings first. So far, I've covered five subjects: Property, Contracts, Constitutional Law...blah, blah, blah." Whatever happened, I knew I had to downplay my anxiety and pretend to be in control.

I needed a mental break—but there was no time for that. This test had become my alpha and omega. My pulse had stopped the day I started law school. It would not beat again until the Board of Law Examiners admitted me to the bar and assigned my attorney practice number.

After three months, the sleepless nights and constant studying were nearly done. The bar exam was days away. I'd done everything I could to prepare myself, but that empty feeling nudged me that it was not enough.

Still, it was too late to switch gears. I drove an hour away to Lansing where the Michigan bar exams were held. The whole way out there, I listened to my Kaplan tapes. I could have had better company with one of my law schoolmates but I told her she couldn't ride with me because I needed to stay focused. Riding with friends would be a distraction. I had to do things the way successful people had told me to, and veering from their advice would cost me the bar.

I arrived one week before the exam and checked into a hotel. My plan was to familiarize myself with the lay of the land, planning every little detail from where I would park my car, down to the BIC pen and Ticonderoga pencil I would use to fill in the bubbles.

The dress rehearsal was smooth. No one was at the test site when I arrived. I roamed freely through the building, peering through the windowpanes of locked doors. After wandering the hallways for a while, I found my designated testing room. I stood on my tiptoes to peek at the endless rows of long, rectangular tables and chairs. "I wonder where my seat is," I murmured and tried the doorknob. *Shoot.* It was locked.

Back at my hotel, I opened my suitcase and reached for my flashcards. There were almost a thousand of them. *Contracts, Torts, Personal Property, Real Property, Family Law, Estates, and Trusts.* My eyes squinted and scrolled over the endless facts, hoping something would stick to my full brain.

Instead, I kept batting at gnats.

I'm not trying to lay out a metaphor for my difficulty with my studies. *Literal gnats* were swarming my room, tiny little biting flies that landed on my face and bit at my neck and ankles. I batted them away, but they just kept coming, a maddening war I was doomed to lose. Before the clock struck midnight, my head was stuffed under the covers, safely tucked away from the swarms of biting flies. My routine was the same for the next two nights. Finally, on Monday, I'd had enough.

Pursuing the invading hordes with a can of bug spray, I found myself in the bathroom. I lifted a loose floorboard and hundreds of gnats swarmed out. I dashed out of the bathroom in horror, slamming the door behind me. *You've GOT to be kidding me.*

I called the front desk. They offered to spray the room. "You don't understand," I told them. "I've *been* spraying the room. It doesn't work." Then I lost my temper. "Do you understand that the bar exam is *tomorrow?* I need to study! What else can you do?"

There was complete silence on the other end of the phone.

"H-E-L-L-O?!" I snapped. "I need to get back to my studies and get rest to prepare for my—you know what?" I changed course. "Let me talk to your manager." I'd had enough of this going-nowhere conversation. This gnat stampede had to *end.*

The manager came on the phone. "Hello, ma'am?"

"Yes. This is *unacceptable.* The spray isn't working, these gnats are all over the room, and I can't study. Even this phone call is taking too much time from my studies—" I started to spiral. Then I took a deep, shaky breath. "Please," I begged. "I need to finish studying and rest for the BAR. I do not have all night."

There was a clicking sound on the other end of the line. "I understand, ma'am. Just give me one second to check on something, and I'll be right back to you."

This irritated me even more, but I reluctantly agreed. A second later, the manager came back to the phone. "Our system shows that we do have *one* room free that we could move you to," he offered.

Already, I could feel my tension release. "How soon can I move?" I asked.

"The bellman is on his way to you now."

Switching to a new room at 8 pm, the night before sitting for the bar, wasn't a part of my meticulous study plan. Nevertheless, the bellman arrived to help me with my bags. He led me to a different floor with much nicer carpets, in an area that didn't look like it was even part of the same shabby hotel where I'd been staying.

I opened the door to the room, and my stress levels instantly subsided. I had landed the presidential suite!

There was a wide-open living space with a separate office. The refrigerator was filled with delectable snacks, and a coffee bar offered a range of roasts and syrups. There was a California king-size bed, and even a massive jacuzzi bath! The whole room screamed R-E-L-A-X!

And I was happy to obey. Thrilled to have a bathing area that didn't involve standing on a wooden floor cavity full of swarming gnats, I ran the bath water, got in, and instantly fell asleep. It was the first time I had relaxed in years.

That jacuzzi saved my life, but it also probably contributed to my failing the bar the first time.

12

Lonely, Not Alone

"The moment you move independently of God, you have moved away from the treasure within."

—TONY EVANS

*O*nce the bar exam was behind me, I was finally able to re-engage with people. Exhausted and driving in the dark, I decided to call Mom on the way home. That's when she told me a distant family member, my cousins' mother, had passed away.

"Oh, no! How are the kids doing?"

"They're taking it hard. The funeral is this coming Saturday. Let me know if you're going to make it," she said.

Needless to say, my plans for a little mind break did not go as planned. I was slammed back into reality with a death in the family. Although my aunt-in-law and I weren't close, I felt awful for her children—I couldn't imagine the pain my cousins were feeling with the sudden loss of their mother. But I was too mentally drained and exhausted to call them. Instead, I dialed the number for Wesley.

Wesley and I started dating long-distance soon after I started the JD-MBA program. He was launching his own consulting business, and typically, he was just as busy as I was. That night, as I drove home from the bar exam, he was on a work deadline. "Can't talk, babe," he told me, answering his phone on the fifth ring. "Call you tomorrow."

Anyone grinding and committed to their profession is admirable. But that day, he annoyed me. I wanted to celebrate my accomplishments with loved ones, but no one seemed to care.

"Why isn't my phone ringing right now?" I grumbled to myself. "Everyone was blowing it up when I was studying, and now that I'm done, they don't even call and congratulate me."

I turned on Stevie Wonder, but even his genius did little to lift my mood. I decided to focus on driving down that dark, slippery road. *Everyone's too busy for me, anyway.*

This journey was mine and mine alone.

When I got home, I crashed. I'd put everything I had into that test. The results wouldn't be published for a few months. *Now what?* All I could do was lie in my bed, sulk, and sleep. Thankfully, I had some time off from work to rest. The sun would not shine on my face for days. The most I moved was from the bed to the refrigerator.

I was a couch potato—or more like a *bed* potato, if that's a thing. Lying in bed, I let my thoughts run wild. I'd imagined this moment differently. This was supposed to be *my* time. *I put in years of hard work, and no one cares.* My phone did not ring. The gloom of my dark room matched my dismal mood.

I laid in bed for the rest of the week, until it was time for me to return to work. I mustered enough energy to find a wrinkle-free, easy outfit to throw on for those first eight hours. My corporate smile masked the hurt I felt on the inside. *Confusion.* I had no idea what I was supposed to do now. The plans I had written for myself were accomplished. My plans stopped after taking the bar exam, as I assumed I'd pass on the first try. When would I know whether I'd passed? And what was I supposed to do now?

Immersed in my negative thoughts, I recalled the beginning of law school. That bright-eyed young lady who went to church regularly was no longer here. The Mileka who had a strong relationship with God had ceased to exist.

And while thinking long and hard about my constant state of depression, I had an epiphany.

As soon as I got my foot into law school, I'd checked God at the door. He had gotten me through so much, and I'd turned my back on our relationship. Giving God the peace sign, signaling *I have it from here, Lord, I'll see you later*, was what had landed me in this state of funk.

"Listen to music," Mom suggested. She assured me it would help my mental state. I was trying to hide my sulking, but my mother sensed my tone. She noticed that I wasn't swinging by Muri Hill as I'd done each day faithfully over the years.

> **❝** Giving God the peace sign, signaling I have it from here, Lord, I'll see you later, was what had landed me in this state of funk.

Moping around one evening, I turned on a CD that Dad had let me borrow and began humming to "Amazing Grace" by Mahalia Jackson to soothe my agonized soul. A tear rolled down my face as I remembered that this song had brought me into close fellowship with God a long time ago. He touched my heart, and that day in March, He let me know that I wasn't alone.

Each day brought a little more sunshine. I fought to reclaim my peace of mind. It was tiring, but worth it. Little by little, I came back to myself as God placed a new song in my heart. Singing restored some joy. I wasn't out of the woods yet, but I kept moving. I had a trip coming up, which gave me something to look forward to. In April, I'd set off to France.

13

Journey of Spark

"In order to change the world, you have
to get your head together first."

—JIMI HENDRIX

*O*nce I boarded my flight, I pulled out my journal to get out some of the feelings I had bottled up inside. I felt a little spark. In Paris, I was determined not to spend my vacation in bed. Taking the advice of the concierges at my boutique hotel, I got out and explored. It was uplifting to get a little fresh air, and there was music in the streets. I walked around to the different shops, ate *crêpes*, and even caught the metro. At one point, I found myself lost and unable to read the street signs, but I was saved by an English-speaking woman who guided me back to my hotel.

The first night, I took a dinner cruise alone with my thoughts. The mental struggle was real. I tried to admire the beautiful architecture passing by on the banks of the Seine, but my thoughts were filled with despair. There were a few couples and a family having some kind of celebration with their grandfather.

> " Being alone all the time isn't good for you; everyone needs someone.

He reminded me of my grandfather, Poppy, who encouraged my educational journey but had passed the year I started law school. The older man noticed I was alone, and he came over to my table.

"What's a nice-looking young lady doing here all by herself?" he asked in accented English. My slight smile prevented the tears from rolling down my face.

"Just enjoying the view," I answered.

With a bright, infectious smile, he said, "Don't stay by yourself too long. That isn't good for you; everyone needs someone." He went on to tell me that his family had brought him there to celebrate his 95ᵗʰ birthday. I wished him a happy birthday and assured him I would not be alone too long.

A few days later, I was off to Rome to meet other alumni and students on the MBA's annual international trip. We attended seminars, went shopping, and caught the bullet train to Florence. On the bullet, we snapped pictures of each other falling asleep. When we weren't goofing around, we had intelligent, meaningful conversations about how we were segregated, even in Europe. The Black students hung tight, and the white students flocked together. We all felt an undercurrent of hostility. That was just part of the school's culture.

> 66 Race tensions were evident, and when the conversation turned to diversity in the workplace, I couldn't hold back.

It still seemed to me that the white students looked down on their Black classmates, and a few acted flat-out racist. They weren't interested in getting to know their Black peers. This silent hostility loomed until, one day, the hosting professor brought it up.

We were on the bus heading to one of our many jam-packed events. Race tensions were evident, and when the conversation turned to diversity in the workplace, I couldn't hold back.

"What are you *talking about?*" I asked my classmates. "You blah, blah, blah about diversity, but this whole trip has been white people with white people, Black with Black. How many of you even know everybody's *name?*"

I can't say that outburst won me any new friends, but I didn't let it bother me. For the most part, I was focused on the common ground I felt with our tour guide. She was Egyptian, and she called me "sister." I was intrigued by the sites in Rome, especially the images engraved on the catacombs. All those sacrificial saints whose skin was sun-kissed and bronzed!

The Vatican, unfortunately, wasn't so welcoming. When another MBA alumna and I tried to re-enter the basilica after going to the restroom, one of the guards stepped out to block us. *"Scarafaggi!"* he yelled, which means "cockroaches." Let's just say we didn't need to speak Italian to understand his point of view.

We played it off as if his comments weren't cruel, and we carried on about our day. And even with the occasional nasty encounter, that trip made me better. I was feeling lighter all around: graduation was just around the corner.

Only a handful of students were graduating from the dual-degree program, and I was one of them. Both graduations were scheduled to take place on the main campus of Detroit Mercy. This was full circle for me. Nearly ten years ago, I'd been a regular on this very campus, working towards my Bachelor of Arts degree.

Returning to my undergraduate school made me think back on what I'd learned about academia. Over the years, I'd soaked in what my professors had said about creating an impact, giving back, and making a difference in the world. But their actions had belied their noble words. Dr. Ida, that

English professor who gave my hard-earned A's to a white student. That nasty financial aid advisor, Darby, who'd advised me to drop out when I was almost at the finish line. The countless white students who were mostly inexperienced with Black people but constantly asserting themselves as authorities on our community.

None of them were bad people, as far as I knew. They gave back to the less fortunate, as they'd labeled us Detroiters. They worked at soup kitchens; they mentored youth. They checked the boxes to get their community service hours filled.

Nearly ten years later, I couldn't find any Black students when I walked the halls of the three-story law school and peered at images of alums from as early as the 1900s. Even the old photographs whispered that people with my skin tone did not belong. Yet I wore my robes and walked that stage, proud of my accomplishments.

As always, my family showed up for my graduation. Taven sat right in front, cheering me on. I was proud to have accomplished this for us. He was likely glad that our hectic lifestyle was coming to an end.

Graduation was in the afternoon, and Titan Hall was packed. If my mom's whistle was any indication, I was destined for greatness. As the minister of ceremonies called my name, my supporters' cheers blazed my ears and stretched a gleeful smile across my lips. My judge-like black robe had two velvet stripes on each arm, and my graduation tam crowned my flat-ironed hair. I was now a distinguished JD-MBA graduate.

After the ceremony, families all congregated outside. My parents met me with flowers. My siblings were there, as was Taven, and other family and friends. This was the celebration I had needed after my classwork was completed in December, and it was what I'd been looking for after sitting for the bar. The time was now, though. We snapped pictures, exchanged hugs, and congratulated the other graduates—especially the other Black graduates, as we were familiar with their grit. We floated on cloud nine. We capped off the evening with a nice early dinner. I couldn't stay out late because I had a second graduation for my MBA in the morning. By the end of the night, I was floating in pure bliss.

When I got home, I walked onto the porch, reached into the mailbox, and saw a large white and green envelope. I started tearing it open as soon as I got in the house. I plopped on my couch, hunched over, elbows pressed against my knees, lips pursed. I took a deep breath and pulled the pages out.

FAILED!!!

That word was written a handful of times on the single page notice. The Board of Law Examiners must have thought I was so slow that they needed to repeat my failure again and again, just so the message would sink in. My heart pounded as I slumped back on the couch. My queenly robe no longer suited me. I sat paralyzed in thought, knowing that I was a failure.

It's crazy how happy I'd been that day, only to have the rug of my magic carpet ride yanked right out from under me. That day taught me to enjoy life's moments because everything can change in an instant.

The next morning, I found enough energy to go through the motions of my MBA graduation. When I arrived back on the main campus, the smiles of my enthusiastic classmates lifted my heart as I played along in their joyous moments.

Today was the long-awaited day to celebrate all our hard work. I had to conceal my doom and gloom from them, so I greeted my classmates in kind. We snapped selfies, hugged, and chatted, but all I could think was, *Why would anyone want to celebrate with me? I'm a failure.*

> **"** That day taught me to enjoy life's moments because everything can change in an instant.

My entire family showed up again. I kept my bad news to myself; I couldn't ruin everyone's day by broadcasting the fact that all my endeavors had been for naught. I sat numb during the ceremony. As the master of ceremonies delivered her speech, I felt myself detach from the world.

What are you going to do now? See, you really don't belong here. You wasted all that time getting an education. Your lifestyle will never change because you don't have what it takes to be a lawyer, so why even try again? You're a failure and a fraud.

My self-criticism was harsher than anything anyone had ever said to me. There was no more fight in me that day. My negative mindset had won. I felt hopeless. Everything was over for me. No plan. No future. The JD and MBA were useless.

I told myself to play along and pretend that I was happy since my family deserved some good news. I'd given enough heartache to my parents, and brought enough empty days to my son—so we celebrated.

> 66 I'd given enough heartache to my parents, and brought enough empty days to my son—so we celebrated.

The storm from my tears was mighty that evening. Lying on my bed, staring at the ceiling, my mind flooded with every negative thought imaginable. *What will people think of me? I must not be that smart. What a fool to believe I could pull this off.*

14

Accept Failure

"The greatest glory in living lies not in never failing, but in rising every time we fall."

−NELSON MANDELA

*F*inally, I accepted the four-point hurdle standing in the way of me and my future law practice. I gathered the courage to pick up the white and green envelope again and read through the appeal process, sinking further into my brown leather loveseat as I opened the packet. The pages of the appeal blurred together through the tears streaming down my face. My heart stopped beating. The petition seemed straightforward, but the board of law examiners had just changed the grading that year, so I had to spend some time deciphering the new scoring system. I asked the Examiners to send me an appeal packet, which included my essays along with their model answers to each subject.

> " My wounds were fresh, and the salt kept pouring—but my family continued to support me.

About a week later, the exam results were published, and my failure was outed: everyone in the legal community knew I had failed. I brought my family up to speed. My wounds were fresh, and the salt kept pouring—but my family continued to support me.

"You've got to fight, Mileka," my mother urged. "It's just a few points."

After I'd combed through each essay, comparing it to the model answer, I was convinced that I had enough points to prevail on appeal. The deadline to file was close. At that time, I didn't have a printer, but there was one at my parents' house. I had to spend a night or two on Muri Hill to type and print out my appeal.

Locked away in my childhood bedroom, I redrafted the edits as Mom proofread my essays. She was in and out of the room, carrying on with her life's tasks. I didn't have a minute to spend on anything else, and I mean *anything*—not a shower, not food. Nothing. Mom made sure I ate when I wasn't drafting and reading the printed pages.

The appeal needed to be perfect, and the quick turnaround nearly drove me to despair. But appealing was more attractive than having to sit again for the rapidly approaching July bar. I finished my appeal on the night it was due, and I punched the gas to make the post office in time. Minutes before they closed, I got it in the mail—timestamped just before the deadline.

Weeks passed. Finally, the EXAMINERS acknowledged they had received my appeal and that I should expect something soon. By then, it was early June. Waiting for their reply was purgatory.

Just shy of a month before the July bar, I got another official piece of mail from the board of law EXAMINERS. Breathless, I ripped open the envelope. Scanning the paper, I was certain that the calculation telling me I had four raw points would get me the score I needed—but it was still two points less than what I needed to be an attorney in Michigan. *This is bull crap. It's unfair; how could they not find any more points on appeal—the graders must have rushed through my assessment.* I looked for any reason to console myself, for now, I was faced with a second bar exam.

The next four weeks were consumed with defeating that Goliath. Two points away meant I only needed to make some minor adjustments to pass. A friend of mine named Nicole was studying for the first time, and she'd arranged for a newly admitted attorney, Dawn, to help her with the prep. She invited me to join the sessions, and I couldn't turn down the chance.

We met at her house. There we sat at Nicole's wooden dining room table, accompanied by my array of used Kaplan books and her stacks of fresh Barbri material.

"Where do we start?" she asked.

"Maybe we should make a schedule," I said.

"I say we handle certain topics on each day and, on that day, do both essays and practice multiple choice."

I looked at her, thumbing the edges of my book. Her suggestion was a lot more drastic than the approach I had followed before. "Let's just agree on the days we study together and select the topics for those days," I suggested. We went round and round discussing study methods, without ever formulating a plan. We were still deadlocked when Dawn sashayed in to start our session. Decked out in a colorful, flowing sundress, she looked like she'd been pampering herself after her recent success with the bar. Dawn backed up Nicole, and each of them argued their case about why their method was tried and true.

Then, out of nowhere, Dawn bailed on us, expressing that she'd die if she spent another minute reviewing bar material. She offered all her notes and her number to call with questions.

"I'm sorry, I just can't sit through another session," she declared as she headed for the door less than an hour after she'd arrived.

Tutorless, Nicole and I forged ahead. The sun never kissed me that month. I was indoors 24/7. Once, we tried studying on the patio. The breeze was refreshing, but it soon scattered our papers and notes. After ten minutes or so, we headed back inside. That was my single "fresh-air" moment of the summer.

I was clinging to my old study habits, convinced I needed just two more points to pass, while Nicole tried to pry those old habits from my grip. But the truth is, she learned differently than me. Needing to see a rule only once, her photogenic memory would master it. Her recall was remarkable. I, on the other hand, still in mourning from my failure, struggled through my brain fog and fumbled through the topics. I knew bits and pieces, but not the in-depth cases as they would appear on the test.

"You're conflating the rules, Mileka," Nicole pointed out.

"No, I'm not; see, it's right here." I showed her the rule in my book. She gently tried to explain my mistakes, especially concerning constitutional law, which was her favorite. But entrenched as I was in my "two points to pass" arrogance, I never fully listened to her explanations. The third time she accused me of "conflating," I slapped down my book on the table.

"What does that even *mean*?" I burst out. "Please stop saying that!"

She showed me grace, even though I was belligerent. I was also snippy, frustrated, and fatigued, and she was stuck on the receiving end of my ire. One time, seeing that I needed a break, she got up and walked to her adjoining kitchen. "Want a salmon salad?" she offered.

Eating, like any other essential, was secondary to me. The thought of anything home-cooked was appealing. "Sure! You're going to make that now?"

"Yep, it's an easy meal. You can quiz me while I'm cooking."

I grabbed one of our giant study books and chose a random topic—Property. "Tell me the rule for replevin." And she did, exactly as it was laid out in our textbook.

"Tell me what's needed for eminent domain."

When she answered, I was impressed. "Unbelievable. That's what it says in the book, *word for word.*"

We went through topic after topic as she chopped the lettuce, tomatoes, and red onions. Searing the salmon with a spatula in her hand, she recited the law as if she'd written it herself.

"You're going to pass this test," I said as she placed the salad in front of me. "And this looks delicious." We gobbled our salads, then hit the books again, calling it quits after three more hours of studying.

Down to the wire, we studied every topic—or almost. There's one area called secure trans, which handles creditors' rights against debtors and the rest of the world. It wasn't an area of law that I wanted to practice, and it was rarely tested on the bar. It was low on my priority list to master.

But Nicole was adamant that we should at least review the material. She liked to bring it up after hours of studying when my brain was already twisted. I didn't want to do secure trans, and I told her so. The hour hand was ticking down on the bar and I wanted to stick to the major subjects.

One week away from the test, she brought it up again. "We need to at least look at secure trans." It was midnight, and my eyes were glazed over by the pile of constitutional law notes stacked in front of me.

"If you say that again, I'm going to slap you," I threatened. Silence filled the room. The minutes that passed felt like hours, and I knew I'd gone too far.

She took a deep breath and, in her patient, firm voice said, "Mileka, we are going to have a problem if secure trans is on this bar exam."

"It won't be, trust me. Let's focus on the highly tested areas and we'll be fine." Finally, she conceded. But I could tell from her tone of voice that if I was wrong, we would have an issue.

After a few short weeks of study, the day was here. I'd taken that hour-long drive solo back to Lansing. This time, I would type the test instead of writing it in longhand. The Michigan State University stadium was filled with hundreds of bar takers. It was cold, so I wore white cotton socks with shiny black pointed-toe dress shoes, some jeans, a T-shirt, and a sweater on top. I was seated by the time Nicole got there, but she picked me out of the crowd right away.

"Mileka, is that you?" She started laughing. "You look like Michael Jackson by way of the feet." I glanced down at my feet, and I actually did. The bar exam had me so shaken that my appearance was the least of my worries. I couldn't help but laugh. Nicole walked up to me and reminded me what a monster I'd been during our studies. "Secure trans better not be on this exam," she warned, giving me her sternest look.

"It won't be, don't worry," I reassured her. She walked over to her seat, and the proctor passed out the exams and started the clock.

I peeled the seal off the exam question book, opening it to Page One. And there it was: the one subject I was confident wouldn't be tested. Secure trans was the very first question on the exam. My gut clenched. I turned my head to face Nicole, who sat three rows behind me. She just blinked her eyes and shook her head. My chest was heavy from steering her wrong, but I'd take her eye roll. I knew what she *wanted* to do was slap me.

I turned back around and did my best to limit the damage. I started typing the few rules I knew on secure trans, without any confidence that I had it right. *I'll get at least a few points for this essay*, I thought. *I have to.*

Then I moved on to typing the remaining 14 essays. My words were clumsy and my thoughts were unclear. The keyboard was failing me. *Why did you type?* I chastised myself. *You should have just stuck to writing. You hate typing exams!*

I kept fiddling with the computer, taking more time with the keyboard than I would have with paper and pen.

I turned in my completed exam with minutes to spare, but inside I was hollow. The second day of the exam was the same. Diligently, I filled in 100 multiple-choice questions in the morning, and 100 more in the afternoon. *Done.* I turned in my booklet and headed back to Detroit, agonizing over whether or not I had passed. I had no idea if I'd studied enough.

15

Wait It Out!

"You can't start the next chapter of your
life if you keep re-reading the last one."

—MICHAEL MCMILLIAN

*I*n late fall 2014, Taven and I were in the kitchen, talking as I made dinner. He was excited to tell me about the clothing line he was thinking of creating, and I was proud that he was following his creative passion. As the spaghetti cooked on the stove, I grabbed the pile of mail from the week.

I was partially paying attention to Taven's master plan when I ripped open the white and green envelope. Haphazardly, I opened my bar results. All I saw was "Failed." Determine to keep enjoying our night, I didn't tell Taven. Instead, I balled up the paper and took my Shack free throw towards the trash.

The next day at work, a quiet whisper hissed through the office. All of my co-workers knew that I'd failed, but no one knew how to console me.

A few people tried. The head of our group, the Associate General Counsel, made it his business to stop and chat with me periodically. The first time I failed, he'd come down and encouraged me to go at it again. Now, when he approached me, I wanted to crawl under my desk.

"Have you gotten the results?" he asked.

I mustered up the energy to tell him I hadn't passed again. "I thought God and I had things straightened out," I joked, "but I guess we've got a bit more to discuss." He laughed, lifting my spirits a little.

Another top lawyer at the company, Allyson, took me to lunch. "Don't beat yourself up about it," she told me. "The world does plenty of that already, don't help them."

I confessed to my mentor Jon that I was thinking about not sitting again. I just wasn't convinced I could do it, and the time sacrifice loomed heavy before me. "It's your choice, Mileka," he said, "but I believe in you." Later that week, I got a CD in the mail from him, a sermon titled *"Failure Is Not Final."*

My first mentor Angela also chimed in. She wasn't as gentle as Jon, but she sent me a card titled *"Go Confidently in The Direction of Your Dreams."* I hung that card on my hallway mirror, and I listened to Jon's CD every day. But even with all their encouragement, I wasn't sure I could put myself through that ordeal again.

> 66 What a wasted life— living to prove others wrong instead of developing God-given gifts.

My head was full of worrying about how other people viewed my failures. It was a habit I'd developed early in life. For some reason, I thought the best way to prove myself was to prove others wrong. What a wasted life—living to prove others wrong instead of developing the gifts that God gave me. Even though I was starting to realize my mistake, shaking the world's perceptions wouldn't happen overnight. It was up to me to reclaim myself and discover who I was created to be.

Now I realize how damaged my thinking was. I joke about having a lapse of sanity when I enrolled in the MBA program, but my mental well-being had been bludgeoned long before then.

Being a 17-year-old mother brings trauma. When I was still growing into the person I would become, I had another human being who relied on me to know more than I knew, to be more than I was, and to give more in life than I had to give. As a teenage mother, I teetered on the brink, but my family kept me grounded. Without my parents' love and guidance, I would have perished.

All my life, I'd pursued that empty motto: *Don't be a statistic*. I had no idea what that even meant. It's just a phrase I picked up, back when I was a child in Eye On The Future. While I pursued my ambitious education, common sense had fallen by the wayside. I thought I just had to power through the challenges, and everything in my life would improve. I would be accepted among the self-proclaimed "successful" people—all I had to do was work harder and be better.

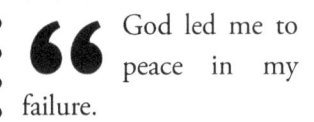

God led me to peace in my failure.

That was all such a shallow way of thinking. Don't get me wrong, aiming to be the best version of yourself is the goal. But setting arbitrary standards about working harder than our white counterparts, or working ourselves into oblivion, is a fool's errand. At least, it was for me. Those goals left me empty. I was working harder than anyone I knew, and by the time I failed the bar a second time, I was about to push myself right off the cliff.

Finally, I took incremental steps toward a better way of thinking. 2014 was the year I began to repair from teen-mom trauma, and began finding my place in this world. Having to sit again after learning I'd failed the first time flung me into despair. And failing a second time cast a dark cloud over me that shadowed my every movement. But then I got an opportunity to write...and the clouds started to open.

I volunteered to write the Christmas play for our local church. That gave me life. I read my scriptures over and over again until I had the idea of setting my script in the present day. I wrote before work, I thought about the play during the day, and I wrote in the evenings and on weekends. I was happy and in my zone. The stress of having failed my second bar exam faded to the back of my mind. My focus was on writing the production and co-laboring with God. I felt revived.

> **"** In reality, writing saved me from the darkest place I'd ever known.

Little by little, I began to understand that I was more than the skill of passing the bar exam. I reconnected to the things I had enjoyed as a child. Immersed in my work, I found refuge in writing and producing. God led me to peace in my failure, and I now had the choice to sit for the bar again or pivot. But that decision could wait until the production was completed.

I held auditions for the main parts, assembling a choir to perform a musical, youth dancers, and a flag worship scene for my very own mother to play. Plus, my mother's crafty skills enabled us to build props and sew costumes together from scratch. We rehearsed three times a week, and I knew our show was lit. I'd made up my mind to focus on the production, then enjoy the holidays with my family and my beau, Wesley. That was no small thing: I was beginning to carve out boundaries for myself. Little by little, I was appreciating the person God created without fearing what others had to say about me.

Obviously, to some, my work on the production was just playing around. In reality, writing that play saved me from the darkest place I'd ever known. That play was my place of peace, helping me collect my thoughts to refocus. Failing the bar exam wasn't a testament to my intrinsic worth. It was a necessary step in helping to build my character, drive, and determination to continue forward.

Having granted myself some mental space, other people's opinions stopped affecting me the way they had before. Their comments meant nothing. The light bulb finally clicked in my head: I had done all this alone. No one else sat in those classrooms with me, at the law school and the business school. It was *I* who was running my son up and down 96 freeway from Redford to his high school in downtown Detroit. It was *me* buying extra-large cups of Speedway Coffee before school to stay awake so I could participate in class. It was me who had taken the bar not once, but twice—and I had the scars on my heart to prove it.

I had everything I needed when I was born, but the world told me that was not enough. Since then I'd traveled down a trail of lies, and now I had to pivot to get back to my starting place. I *alone* had gotten myself into this conundrum, and I, with God's help, was the only way out.

I was standing at my life's crossroads. Which was the right path to take?

Wesley, who is now my husband, had such belief in me that it was almost annoying. At first, I couldn't accept his supportive words; I was too busy savoring the comments from the nay-sayers. He refused to listen to my reasoning as I predicted that I might not pass the bar on the third try. He gave me speeches from *The Art of War,* telling me to "be like the water" and "flow with the test." I smirked and held back my snippy remarks, but Wesley refused to give up.

> What God wants for me shouldn't be this hard. *Really?*

"You will take the test as many times as you need to pass the bar," he said.

I rolled my eyes. "That's easy for you to say, you're not the one taking the test. Besides, I have a business degree that I can use; my juris doctorate is enough."

"You will sit for the bar and pass it no matter how long it takes," he repeated.

Is he listening to me? I was at my wit's end. I kept reiterating that I had two graduate degrees and a fading desire to become an attorney. But Wesley wasn't having it. His confidence wore on my last nerve!

After all, it was *I* who had endured the grueling schedule in law school, juggling four educational institutions to accomplish a dream. By the time I found out about my second failure, I was mentally depleted. There wouldn't BE a third time because I had finally come to my senses.

But then, there was my mom. She also helped me to discover what I wanted. One day after church, my pastor greeted the parishioners as he normally did after service. He knew I was sitting for the bar again and that I had already failed once. In passing, he asked if I had gotten my results. Gripped with shame, I lowered my eyes and whispered, "I failed."

I was expecting words of comfort, but that's not what he had to offer. "If it's that hard for you," he told me kindly, "then maybe you need to spend some time in prayer about what God wants for you."

I couldn't believe it. *Is Pastor telling me that God wants me to give up?* Before I could ask him to clarify, another parishioner whisked him away. I stood there devastated, and that's when Mom approached.

"You okay, Mileka?" she asked, noticing my trembling chin.

"Maybe being a lawyer isn't for me, like Pastor said. What God wants for me shouldn't be this hard. And I failed twice! That's a clear sign," I sobbed.

She squeezed my hand. "I don't know why he said that to you, Mileka. He should have encouraged you to keep going." She was upset for me, but helped me not to dwell on his comment.

Later that day, I got a call from my law school friend, Kerline. She got an earful about what my Pastor had said. And I gave her every reason why I should quit.

"I know that feeling, but you have to sit again."

"This bar has taken my life away. It's not *worth* it. As Pastor said, maybe I'm on the wrong path. I could have been on the wrong path all along!"

"Don't concern yourself with that right now. You're too close to finishing."

"I don't think I can sit again. It's too much."

"You *can* sit again, and you will. Trust me. If you weren't meant to be an attorney, worry about that after you pass the bar. You can't get distracted trying to figure that out at this point."

> **"** If you weren't meant to be an attorney, worry about that after you pass the bar.

"But what he said is weighing heavy on me. It's solidifying what others want me to believe about myself."

"Listen, you can't worry about what your pastor said, and you can't worry about what other people are saying."

I took a deep, shuddering breath. "You're right."

"Just focus on the bar. I know it seems like all you've done is study, study, study for a year straight. So you know the material! Now you have to practice, practice, practice, and soon you'll be practicing law."

Kerline was right, and I thanked her. And later that day, when I got home, my son had some words for me, too. "What are you going to do, quit? That's not an option, Ma. Three times a charm."

My handsome son who I gave birth to when I was just a child myself encouraged me to keep trying. His four-word phrase, "Three Times a Charm," became my mantra on the third go-round. It reminded me of another poem Mom taught me.

KEEP GOING

"When things go wrong, as they sometimes will,
When the road you're trudging seems all uphill,
When the funds are low and the debts are high,
And you want to smile, but you have to sigh,
When care is pressing you down a bit,
Rest if you must—but don't you quit.

Life is queer with its twists and turns,
As everyone of us sometimes learns,
And many a failure turns about
When he might have won had he stuck it out;
Don't give up, though its pace seems slow,
You may succeed with another blow.

Often the goal is nearer than it seems
To a faint and faltering man.
Often the struggler has given up
When he might have captured the victor's cup,
And he learned too late, when the night slipped down,
How close he was to the golden crown.

Success is failure turned inside out—
The silver tint of the clouds of doubt,
And you never can tell how close you are,
It may be near when it seems so afar;
So stick to the fight when you're hardest hit—
It's when things seem worst that you mustn't quit."

EDGAR GUEST

16

Three Times a Charm

"The real test is not whether you avoid this failure, because you won't. It's whether you let it harden or shame you into inaction, or whether you learn from it; whether you choose to persevere."

—BARACK OBAMA

J anuary 2, 2015. I opened my bar prep books, the words already blurred through the puddles of my tears. *Lord, why do I have to do this again?*

I sat in my cluttered home office, trying not to let my son hear me crying and hating myself for stealing more time away from him. I was now in the darkening trenches, trying to redeem myself and accomplish my dream.

Taven was in the next room, pacing. His nervous footfalls signaled to me that the bar exam had worn out its welcome in our home.

> " I was now in the darkening trenches, trying to redeem myself and accomplish my dream.

Between my tears and the squeak of my son's sneakers on the floorboards, that night was wasted studying. My mind raced, fighting the certainty of my failure. I could not see the light at the end of the tunnel. All I could feel was the cold, drab hole I needed to climb out of.

Other people's words echoed in my head:

"You're going to sit again?"

"It must not be meant for you if you have to work that hard."

"Maybe you need to take some time off. Go at it later on."

Then there were my own self-doubts, harsher than any of my critics:

Will I ever be able to pass the test?

Should I just rely on my graduate and undergraduate degrees?

How will I ever earn more money to create the lifestyle I want?

Why did I even bother going to school?

Lord, why would you let me fail?

No. I shook my head. *I* was in the trenches, and only I could dig myself back to the surface. *I can do this. I deserve to finish what I started.*

As my thoughts calmed, the tears dried and a smile started to reveal itself. I was proud and privileged to sit for the bar. Yes, even for a third time—and in fact, especially then. The only barriers to converting JD to Esquire were my own negative thoughts.

> ❝ The only barriers to converting JD to Esquire were my own negative thoughts.

That day, I came back to myself. I no longer wanted to live for *them*; it was my life, and I had to embrace it. I had to release my internal turmoil about whether I was accepted by others. God made me perfectly acceptable to him, and I needed to see myself through a clearer lens. Finally, I was shifting to a better mindset—one where I believed in myself without thinking, as I had when I was a child in kindergarten.

As my focus shifted, my thoughts turned to the encouraging things people had said to me:

"Failure is not final."

"Go confidently in the direction of your dreams."

"Practice, practice, practice, and soon you'll practice law."

"Be as water with the test. You got this. No matter what it takes, you will become a lawyer."

"Go get your two points."

It took hours before I finally closed my book with a parting thought: *Do it for yourself. You deserve it.*

My wrestling match with God that night was the final break before mending. The load was lifting, and joy began healing my heart. I began to appreciate how the experience of the bar had helped build up my character. I had learned the depths of my fragility. He revealed that to me. There was a brokenness in me that I had masked as my truth.

Honestly, the process of failure taught me how to accept defeat. The mirror was turned to my face and I had nothing to do but stare at it. The image that looked back at me was not all bad. I saw my soul and remembered all the experiences that got me to where I was that day. I was not at the finish line yet. The bar exam was but a blip on the radar, compared to the many things that my faith had allowed me to overcome. My relationship with my Creator beamed brightly in my mind and I knew that my life was not over, even if I failed again. The mountain that was the bar became a molehill that I would easily pass over as I became more reliant on God's guidance.

> " There was a brokenness in me that I had masked as my truth.

That night, God and I made a deal. I pledged that I would give it my all, following His plan. I knew I would fall short, but I trusted God to make up the difference.

This third time would prove to be a radical adventure.

The next day, I began to prepare. My fear of being a forever failure gave me fuel. "You can do this," I said to my reflection in the mirror. "This won't be forever." I wasn't entirely sure yet, but I trusted that God hadn't brought me this far to forget about me. All that failure had to be for a reason.

Sitting for the bar the third time was my sneaky little secret. I needed to set boundaries in place to protect myself from the impending ridicule that I knew would crush my spirit. No one at work knew that I was sitting a third time. I 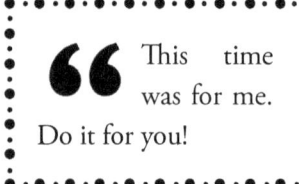 hid my flashcards in my bag, only pulling them out when I was alone on my lunch break. I didn't want anyone's words of advice in my head now. I was focused, and this time was for me. Step One was learning to trust, hear, and follow the direction that God wanted me to take—day-by-day, hour-by-hour, and minute-by-minute. Step Two was learning to trust myself.

This time, my routine was different than it had ever been before. Discipline was in my grasp. I began to let go of the poor study habits that hadn't been serving my goals. I charted out the most highly-tested topics on the exam against my best and worst subjects. After all, I had a lot of material from bars one and two. On that chart, I assigned a subject to each day and stuck to it. That chart was my roadmap through the bar.

At the time, Michigan had 200 multiple-choice questions and 15 essays. Keeping true to Taven's "Three Times a Charm" mantra, I purchased every single old multiple-choice question available from the National Conference of Bar Examiners, and I practiced them religiously. I purchased the online questions from one of the bar preparation companies and practiced those on my phone. For the essays, I printed the old exams, and I practiced them in writing. Although my days were crowded with work, every second was accounted for.

This time, I learned that my ten-to-fifteen-minute television breaks were my biggest distraction from studying, and I unplugged the television. I disconnected from every looming negative thought, every fleeting damaging comment. Whether people were cheering for my success or for me to sink deeper into the quicksand that had become my life, it no longer mattered to me.

Each day, my head lifted toward the sun, strengthening my belief that I would pass with God's grace and help. As this thought grew, the other, negative ideas shrank in the distance. I began to remember the many times that God had carried me before. He'd always met me when I came up short, even after giving my all. With that epiphany, my remaining fears melted away.

About three weeks into bar prep, I got a call from Nicole, who was now a lawyer.

"My friend Jaz wants to study with you," she announced.

Great. That's all I need. "I don't know," I hedged. "You know I'm used to studying alone."

"I know, but I wouldn't recommend it if I didn't think you two would do good for each other—she's really smart, trust me."

I hesitated. *Lord, really?* But eventually, I relented. "I'll try it out to see how it works. I guess there's no harm."

She gave me Jaz's number, so I called her that day to study. I packed my oversize tote with books, highlighters, binders, pens, and Post-its, put on my boots and winter coat, and headed toward the unfamiliar.

Before I could knock, Jaz opened the door to her mini-mansion and greeted me with her bubbly personality. *That's a lot of house for a young woman,* I thought. She escorted me to her kitchen, where her books were spread across the table. Jaz was talkative and enthusiastic about the bar, whereas I was drained from overwork and skeptical about group studying. But then she offered me snacks, and I decided I'd give it a go.

For hours we poured over the material, quizzing and learning from each other. Jaz was smart, as Nicole had said. Plus, we complemented each other. She was strong in some areas, and I was strong in others. It was well past midnight when I collected my study materials, put on my coat and boots, and slogged through the frozen weather to head home. There were just a few hours left to rest before I needed to rise, eat breakfast, take my son to school and get to work.

After that first day of studying, Jaz and I worked together most days until the bar exam. It was like we didn't need sleep— our exam adrenaline fueled us. Some nights we studied so late that I fell asleep during our study sessions. She was kind enough to give me her bed, and she took the couch. I'd rest for an hour or so, then head home to follow my morning routine and get ready for work.

During the day, I studied at work in secret. I'd disappear into our vault, where we housed our corporate files. Or else I'd take my phone in the bathroom with me to meet my 100-question quota for the day. I was utterly focused on my goal, unencumbered by other people's thoughts and feelings. I shook off the idea that I had to prove my worth to anyone.

Things were going well until one day, my manager Karen shook me. I was taking my lunch break at my desk. My assigned seat was hidden behind a cuBIC le, so I could study discreetly. I had just pulled my practice questions out of their unmarked folder, when Karen poked her head in. Her excuse was that she was dropping off some documents, but she was also being a little bit nosy.

"Oh, I thought you were out to lunch," she remarked, handing me the folder.

I put my arm over my study material, but it was too late.

"You're going to take the test again?" Her eyes widened in surprise. "I don't know if I could sit for the bar more than once."

Her words punched me in the guts. "What am I going to do, quit?"

"Yeah, you have a point—enjoy your lunch!" She walked off. My appetite was gone. I packed up my practice material and headed to the vault. That was the only quiet place I could find at work.

My prep for the third bar felt different, and not just because of my study habits and focus. I felt confident. God let me know that He was right there with me. I knew I was coming up short, but I kept giving my all.

God had carried me in undergrad, when I was so broke that people encouraged me to drop out. He had carried me through my rejection from law school and subsequent appeal. He had carried me when so many people had said that I couldn't, or shouldn't, or didn't belong.

Those tiny miracles paled when I considered how God had rescued me from other real-life situations. He'd reached out His hand to the confused 17-year-old, who was devastated that she was a disappointment to those who believed in her. God had provided for the naive teen mother who scratched her way out of a hole to dual graduate degrees. And now here I was, honored to be sitting for the bar exam.

Somehow along the way, I had forgotten about all this. My tunnel vision of failing the bar had overshadowed everything else in my life. Focusing on my failures made me forget who I was and who I belonged to.

Late one night, I was driving home alone when all these realizations flooded me, and my heart opened to all of God's blessings. My mind shifted to all the positive things I'd overcome. My thoughts rose to embrace what I had accomplished, instead of just the struggle.

> 66 Focusing on my failures made me forget who I was and who I belonged to.

In that midnight hour, my faith was fortified, and I knew I was not alone. Just before I made it home, I said an urgent prayer:

> *"Lord, I thank you for all the times that you have protected me. I thank you for all the blessings that you have given me. I thank you for being here for me even when I turned my back on you. I thank you for this journey. I thank you for keeping my mind focused, and allowing me to sit again for the test. I ask for forgiveness for doubting you.*
>
> *Lord, I am relying on you to get me through this. I know you will carry me as you have before. This, my Lord, is my expectation."*

At that moment, I transitioned from being a lost person into the full knowledge of who I was—even though I didn't fully understand myself yet. Previously, I hadn't fully concentrated on the material to master the test. My mind had been blurred and tangled with how I felt people slighted me, brushing past me as if I were not there. Instead of focusing on what I was doing, I'd been consumed with feeling constantly ignored and isolated. That was a terrible place to live; peace of mind is everything and I had nothing.

After that night in my old Crown Vicky, I resolved that I would focus on the task before me and get it done. I would no longer lift my megaphone to my lips and blast, "Hey everybody look at me, I'm sitting for the bar!" as if to obtain the world's approval. Just as I had learned to step into the deep places of my past failures, I knew that I would win if I listened.

When I sat for the bar the third time, nearly a year after my first attempt, I put my all into it, and I expected a different outcome.

 *"For I know the thoughts I think towards you, saith the LORD, thoughts of peace, and not of evil, to give you an expected end."* Jeremiah 29:11, KJV

This time, I lasered in on the EXPECTED END. "Lord, you promised that you would give me an expected end, so I expect to pass this bar." This third time, I made known my desired outcome, and that's how I proceeded.

Everything that I'd refused to do the first time out of fear that it would mess up my study regimen, I ended up doing the third time. I'd even gone over to Nicole's house so she could drill me on the concepts I was "conflating." Sometimes I didn't get to her house until midnight for our fire drill reviews. I put my bullhorn down and walked into work with my tote bag much lighter, as my practice questions were on my phone. My printed study materials were much smaller. In fact, all I had was my study plan and review schedule. That's all I needed.

The day came for me to sit again, and I was fully at peace. On the drive up, my friend Duane talked the entire ride–NONSTOP. I was proud of myself for not letting any irritation rise up in me. Nothing and no one could disturb my calm, not even Duane chattering in my ear. I just listened and hummed along with Francesca Battistelli singing "He Knows My Name" in the background.

Despite my focus on the music, Duane kept talking. "Funny story about how I got my first management job," he drawled.

There was no out for me; I had to listen. I pretended to be interested. "Really, how did you become a manager? Where was it?"

He started from the top, and soon I knew more than I ever wanted to about every little detail of his career. I sensed this was his way to shake his anxiety, so I didn't dwell on it. I let him speak and tried not to let my humming interrupt his narrative.

The hour breezed by, and before I knew it, we were in Lansing and the test was the very next morning. This time, the room I stayed in was gnat-free. It was peaceful, and I was Zen. I spent time reviewing my flash cards, practicing questions on my phone, and packing my Ziploc bag full of pens, pencils, highlighters, sharpeners, and the Post-it note with my seat number. I'd decided to handwrite this third exam instead of fumbling around with the keyboard and mouse again.

The next morning, I walked into what looked like a large conference room. The proctor sat at the front, before a whiteboard with the time the test would start. I walked down the center row, looking at the seat numbers taped on the desk in front of each seat, passing row after row until finally I got to the front of the class. I was in the first row, and the other test-takers were already there.

"Hello, how are you?" I said to my desk mate. She grinned, annoyed, as she twiddled her pen between her pointer and middle fingers. I let it go. I wasn't there to make friends—I was on a mission. Instead of flying into a tizzy and I usually would, I ignored her flipping pen and popping gum noises.

I focused on the things within my control. I pulled out my black pen and yellow and pink highlighters. I slid the Ziploc bag under my chair and leaned back. When the proctor handed out the exam questions and blue books, I opened my book and inadvertently skipped the first question. "Question One," I wrote in my blue book—but it was actually Question Two.

My index finger traced each word, sentence after sentence, paragraph after paragraph. Then I read the question again, highlighting the key facts in yellow and the issues in pink. The steadiness of my hand revealed to me that I was in a better state than I had been the first or second time around. My answer was so involved it took almost 25 minutes to draft the essay. I continued this routine, tracing my finger under each question as I read it and highlighting the law in yellow and the issues in pink. There were nine questions that morning, and six in the afternoon.

As I turned to what I thought was my final question, I glanced at the round clock in the center of the wall and saw that I had 25 minutes for one more essay. *I'm doing so well.* I drafted my final answer as the test taker in the seat next to me started flipping her pen again. She closed her book, slouched back in her chair, and stared at me in boredom. I glanced at her and held my tongue. I wanted to snap, "What are *you* looking at?" But instead, I reminded myself to focus.

I flipped back to the first page of the exam to see if I could add anything to my essays. It was then, seven minutes before the end of the morning session, that I realized I'd missed the entire first question. Seized with panic, I sped through that question like my pen was on fire. I finished with no time to review my essay before the proctor called, "Time. Pens down!"

That day, I truly gave it my all.

The afternoon session was also a goof. I spent so much time on questions one through five that I only had ten minutes to write the last essay. I finished in silent prayer, "*Lord, I know I fell short and need you to show up.*" The second day of the exam was no different. I ran out of time in the morning and afternoon on the multiple-choice questions. I missed about 20 questions in total because I moved so slowly. All I could do was pray...

> *"Dear God, I need you to carry me because I am coming up shorter than I ever have before. I have peace that I will pass this time because I expect to, and I know you will not let me down. You're letting me run out of time and miss questions so that I will know it is only you. Thank you in advance for this blessing."*

***

After the test, I refused to fall into another depression. Instead, I focused forward. School was in my rear-view mirror. My son was out of high school, so we made the most of it. Even before I received my results, I started applying for better-paying jobs with different responsibilities. This was my way of taking charge of my career and following my own path.

The caterpillar was morphing into a butterfly.

Fly butterfly, fly!

17

Chosen

"We may be overlooked by others but we
are handpicked by God."

–LYSA TERKEURST

*D*uring the two months that I waited for my results, I started appreciating the people in my life again. Taven was still distant, but we found time to eat together and catch up occasionally. My family at Muri Hill continued to welcome me with open arms daily, and I even enjoyed some daylight time with Mom and Dad outdoors.

I continued to work full-time, and each morning I walked into the building with my head held high. I wasn't over the mental sting of failing the bar twice in a row, but I found a way to keep going. I had done everything I knew to pass the exam. I came out of it knowing that if I failed in my own might again, the secret this time was that God would SOMEHOW make up the difference. Therein lay my confidence.

> " The secret this time was that God would SOMEHOW make up the difference.

My colleagues' small slights no longer mattered to me. Finally, I was shifting my energy to the things that I wanted. Instead of telling myself, "See, you failed, you should just give up," and "You do not belong here," I started saying, "Mileka, good job on facing your failures," and "Mileka, you were born for this, and you got this!" Somehow, I actually started to believe what my supporters were saying: "Mileka, you will win!" Nothing changed about my environment, but everything changed about my mindset. No matter how miserable I was dealing with people I thought were snobbish, it wasn't the end for me. I even found a way to forgive them.

Holding animosity towards people—especially those who played minor roles in my life–just wasn't worth my peace of mind. I wouldn't let them hold me back. After all, I believed the Three Winans Brothers' iteration of the Bible verse, "If God Be for Us Who Can Be Against Us." This song was my mantra when I felt like so many were against me. It helped me to say *So what? Those who are for you are greater than those against you.*

Work became easy. I was no longer behind the tall cuBIC le, but in an office now, alongside my paralegal peers. I began

> 66 Nothing changed about my environment, but everything changed about my mindset.

to engage more at work, and spoke freely about whatever topic was on the table. My attorney journey did not have to be the focal point of every conversation. One day in a meeting with Karen and Suzan, we were discussing the rollout of a compliance program that I was leading when my phone kept buzzing on vibrate. After the fifth time, I hurried the meeting along because I needed to see why my friend Tenisha just wouldn't stop calling.

Always suspicious that something bad had happened, I dialed her number with my heart in my throat. "Hey, Tenisha what's going on?"

"Congratulations Counselor!" she yelled into the phone.

"What do you mean?" I responded, getting up to step out of the meeting.

"Congratulations Counselor!" she repeated.

"The results are out?"

"Yes, the seat numbers are posted."

Still in disbelief and doubting that I had passed, I clarified. "How do you know I passed, I thought? Do you have my seat number?"

"Big brother, or in this case big sister, *always* knows."

I pulled up the results on my laptop and scanned the screen. "Tenisha, seriously. I can't find my seat number. Where is it?" I asked, starting to panic.

Poor Tenisha had to sit on the phone while I frantically searched for my seat number. Going through emails was a dead end. It was pure torture not knowing for certain. How could Tenisha be so sure? I had to find out NOW.

What was *my seat number, anyway?* I remembered pulling the number off the table on the last day of the exam, and stuffing the orange index card into my plastic Ziploc bag. It had to still be there. *It has to.*

"Let me get out of here and get the place card. I need to call Taven to pick me up. He dropped me off today."

"Okay, call me when you get the number but until then— congratulations, Counselor!" We both chuckled, but I was still uneasy.

My phone rang again before I could call Taven.

"Hey, Trina!" I greeted my friend. "The results are out."

"I know!" she squealed. "I wanted you on the phone when I checked the list."

Trina and I had started school together and we'd both taken the February 2015 bar. She had it even tougher than me. She worked full-time during her studies, plus she was pregnant. If that wasn't hard enough, she'd also just buried her father. Trina was one of the strongest women I knew. I thought of her as Mighty Mouse.

"Do you have your seat number?" I asked.

"Yes, do you know yours?"

"No, I need to call Taven to pick me up. Let me call you right-right back."

Taven, I need you to pick me up. THE RESULTS ARE OUT 911. Can you come now? He worked across the street at the mall and had only just started his shift.

Mom, I just got here. I can come when I have backup in 45 minutes.

Okay, please hurry. My heart was beating out of my chest. I packed my bags and called out, "See you tomorrow," to my colleagues as I headed for the door.

Three minutes had passed since I talked to Taven. I watched the rainfall in the vestibule as my heartbeat thundered in my chest. Then I remembered I still needed to call Trina back.

She picked up on the first ring.

"Mileka, did you call Taven?"

"Yes but he can't leave Dairy Queen until his co-worker gets there to relieve him. Urrgh! Why can't I leave?" I groaned. "What about you? Did you find your seat number?"

"I did!"

"And? Don't leave me hanging like that; did you look on the list?"

"I looked, and my number's on it! I PASSED!"

I yelled with her like a crazy person, right there in the vestibule of my job. "This is so exciting!" I cheered. "How does it feel?"

"It feels funny, like almost not real. I want to wait until I get the results in the mail to be double-triple sure."

"No way, you got this!" I snatched doubt by the throat as it tried to strangle my friend's moment of celebration. "I'm jumping in the vestibule for you, looking like a mad person, now you need to jump too!" I told her.

And little by little, the reality sank in. Finally, she shouted, "I passed!"

We both yelled and hollered together. It was great to celebrate with my friend. We talked until she had to go and share the wonderful news with her family. I stood watching the rain pour down. I still had 23 more minutes to wait for Taven. I scrolled through the list, hoping I'd magically remember my seat number. It was either 0310 or 0130. My habit of inverting numbers had come back to bite me. I was certain of the four digits, but unsure of their order. Seat number 0310 was on the list, not 0130. I prayed my number was the former, but I was only 70 percent sure.

My belly was jumping with excitement as I waited for Taven.

Then finally, Crown Vicky whipped around the corner. The rain washed me as I ran to the car without an umbrella. "I hope your seat number is on the list, Ma," Taven told me, with typical teenage enthusiasm. "I don't know if I can take another summer with your head stuck in a book." I laughed and told him I wanted this summer to be different too. He didn't have enough time on his break to drive me home, so I drove him back to work before taking the car.

As he got out, I reached for a hug and held him tightly with excitement and childish glee. I kissed his scratchy cheek.

"Good luck, Ma," he said. "Let me know how it goes, I hope 0310's your seat number."

"Me too," I told him, speeding off with 15 more minutes between me and my bar results. I punched Crown Vicky through Dearborn up to Telegraph Road, making it home in record time.

I screeched to a halt, grabbed my tote, and tripped up the steps before fumbling with my keys to get in the house. Still soaking wet from the rain, I ran into the kitchen to get that Ziploc bag. There it was, the bright orange seat card in bold print: 0310. I tripled-checked the list, and there it was, 0310, in plain sight.

I WON!!!

I screamed and yelled, running back and forth through the house. "YES! I PASSED! THANK YOU JESUS, I PASSED!" This craziness went on for ten minutes before I calmed myself enough to share the news.

"Hello, Mom?" My voice was shaking when she picked up the phone. "I need to tell you something. Is Dad there? I need to tell you both at the same time. "

"Yes, he's here, let me get him."

I heard Dad pick up the other receiver on their landline. "Mom, are you there?"

"Yes, I'm here, and so is Dad."

"Wait, give me one second, I need Taven to hear this too. I'll add him to the call."

"Taven?"

"Mom?"

"Dad?"

"I'm here too, Mileka, what's up?" Dad asked, sounding concerned.

"I want you all to know that you are talking to Mileka L. Jonson...Attorney at Law!"

Dad, Mom, Taven, and I yelled in unison. That went on until my voice got hoarse. I let Taven get back to work and told my parents I'd head to Muri Hill to celebrate with them soon.

When I hung up, I called Wesley. Oddly, he picked up on the first ring.

"Hey, babe!"

"How's your day going?" I rasped.

"It's busy today, just about to leave work. What's wrong with your voice?"

"Well, I need to tell you something. You may need to sit down because I have some news."

"Oh Lawd, what's going on?"

"Are you sitting down?"

"Yes. Mileka, seriously, tell me."

"Wesley, you are talking to Mileka L. Jonson, Esquire, AKA Attorney at Law!" I screamed with what little voice I had left. But that didn't matter because he was screaming with me.

"We passed!" he yelled into the phone. *"YES!"*

I called my siblings and close friends to invite them into victory's corner. The excitement was contagious and everyone I called screamed louder.

As I welcomed my tribe in to celebrate my win, I realized that I had shut them out during my defeats. That day, I vowed to be as open with my friends and family in my failures as I was in my triumph. The most important people God had placed in my life were right there, in my corner, and they loved me just the same, with or without this accomplishment.

When Wesley said "We passed," he told me that I was not alone. The screams of Dad, Mom, Taven, Oto, Jayme, Myee, and all my friends were the outpouring I needed to keep me on my path back to myself.

My tribe would help me get there.

18

Life Goes On...

"Your time is limited, so don't waste it living someone else's life. Don't be trapped by dogma—which is living with the results of other people's thinking. Don't let the noise of others' opinions drown out your own inner voice."

–STEVE JOBS

*F*our years after passing the bar, Wesley and I jumped the broom. After we got married, I moved to a different state to live with him. That same year, I'd finally sit with myself long enough to unpack the trauma I'd accumulated while reaching for my dream. I felt compelled to put my experiences on paper, "transcending to the other side of trauma," as my therapist calls it.

> **66** Instead of confronting my trauma, I did what I thought was best: I found the heaviest load I could carry and dragged it behind me under the banner of a dream.

And there was so much trauma. Trauma from having a baby when I was a child. Trauma from the shame I felt for being ill-equipped as a mother. Trauma from having to bury Antony too soon and feeling clueless about how to comfort 10-year-old Taven as he quietly mourned his father's death. Trauma from trying to make up for the loss Taven felt without his dad teaching him how to become a man. Trauma from trying to be a super parent. Trauma from my inauthenticity as I navigated the isolation I felt in mostly white school and work environments. And trauma from years of masking it all.

Instead of confronting my trauma, I did what I thought was best: I found the heaviest load I could carry and dragged it behind me under the banner of a dream. I had to make myself more significant than the image in the mirror staring back at me. Far from avoiding being a statistic, I had become a statistic twice over: both a teen mom, and the mother of a fatherless son.

And so I had fought to prove "them" wrong. I took on whatever looked like a challenge, even when it wasn't my fight. I walked the halls of my law school feeling like the world was against me, and in some respects, it was.

Thankfully, all that cleared up when I realized who my ultimate opponent was: me. That's the realization that finally turned the tide. It had always been me versus me, never me versus them. My legal training taught me what I probably would have learned as a young woman if the call to adulthood hadn't happened so fast: When you get in the boxing ring, have a purpose. Don't swing aimlessly at things that don't matter.

In my case, I learned to stop swinging at thin air around other people's words, which only caused me to view myself negatively. Instead of building up that wall to keep everyone out, I let it come down. During the first year of my marriage, I began creating safe boundaries to protect myself with proper defenses.

I haven't learned it all yet. Perhaps a few more therapy sessions, continuing to actively examine my life, and a few more books will help. For now, I know that what people say about me is none of my concern.

And, as a wise friend, Tamira Chapman, once told me...

God created you great. Who is anyone, including you, to say differently?